Here's The Hambledon Club!

*The Story of Hambledon Cricket Club
1796-2000*

Neil Jenkinson

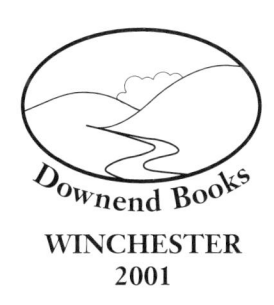

*Supported by
Hampshire
County
Council*

Downend Books

**WINCHESTER
2001**

Copyright 2000 © Neil Jenkinson

All rights reserved. No part of this publication may be reproduced, stored in a retrieval system or transmitted in any form or by any means, electronic, mechanical, photocopying, recording or otherwise without the prior written permission of the copyright owner.

Front cover illustrations:
Long view of Hambledon from the East, 1937 group and modern group.

Contents

Acknowledgements 5
Introduction 7
  1. Hambledon 9
  2. Foundations 13
  3. On Windmill Down 17
  4. Brook Lane 27
  5. Recorded History 29
  6. Turn Of The Century 43
  7. The Route To The Monument 55
  8. Before A Fall 63
  9. Starting Again 69
10. Back In The Public Eye 77
11. After Whalley-Tooker 89
12. More War And A Recovery 97
13. Bowlers and Fund-Raisers 105
14. Desmond Eagar - President 119
15. Open To Competition 127
16. Success in the Leagues 135
17. Natural Popular Favourites 139
18. Nervous Nineties 143
Books and Documents Consulted 151
Index 154

Dedication

To Jilly and Ben who helped

Fill up your glass, he's the best that drinks most.
Here's the Hambledon club; who refuses the Toast?
Let's join in the praise of the bat and the wicket,
And sing in full chorus the PATRONS
OF CRICKET

The Revd Reynell Cotton, 1773

Acknowledgements

I am very grateful to the following who helped in various ways: to Bob Beagley and his sister Marion who made the Hambledon Club's documents available to me and were supportive and helpful throughout: to Chris de Mellow for both information and opinion: to Ida Barrett and Ena Lott for their recollections; A.H. (Podge) Brodhurst, General Hew Butler; to David Frith for permission to reproduce pictures from Pageant of Cricket; John Goldsmith, Roger Heavens and Ronald D. Knight: Lieutenant Commander Charles Lutyens: John May MPS for help with photography: Ken Moon, Ashley Mote: Mrs. Norman for making available files belonging to the late Terry Norman; Dick Orders of The Bat and Ball, Christine Pardoe for photographs, for making available her grandfather's records, for practical assistance and, above all, for hospitality; Andrew Renshaw; Colour World, Olivers Battery, Winchester: Bert Pink, Mrs. Doreen Turner for documents and photographs, Maureen Wingham for access to her collection of photographs, and to my wife Jilly and son Ben for their very practical support.

To the staffs of Hampshire Record Office, Hampshire County Library – Winchester Local Studies, Portsmouth Central Library and the Royal Naval Museum, Portsmouth.

For practical assistance my thanks are due to Councillor F.E. Emery Wallis and Hampshire County Council, MCC and their curator Stephen Green, Lord Alexander of Weedon QC, Dr. Allan Mitchell and Mrs. F.K. Reed. To David Eno Creative Design for putting the book together so elegantly.

Money Values

Comparative values of the pound e.g. Base 1990 £1

Year	Value	Year	Value
1894	£50.47	1950	£13.66
1905	£47.92	1955	£11.00
1914	£43.20	1960	£9.63
1919	£20.05	1970	£6.68
1925	£24.15	1975	£3.93
1930	£27.34	1980	£1.92
1935	£31.75	1990	£1.00
1938	£27.56	1998	£0.75
1946	£16.54		

*Two views of Hambledon at the turn of the century.
Above: The High Street. Below: East Street*

Introduction

This book aims to tell the story of Hambledon Cricket Club between the years 1796 and 2000. The first date is the year when the last act of the classical Hambledon club was recorded: a negative act as the minute book read: no gentlemen.

Apart from a discussion of the date when the club's activities started around 1750, I have not retold the story of the great days and big matches of the XVIII Century. They have already been covered in a scholarly and critical way first by F.S. Ashley-Cooper in 1924 when he published his survey of the minute book and account book of the Hambledon club, and by Ashley Mote in his account of the history of Broadhalfpenny Down, "The Glory Days Of Cricket" published in 1997. I am indebted to both of them but our paths follow different routes.

There are gaps in the story I have to tell: only three matches are recorded between 1794 and 1808, one of them, the "Anniversary Match" advertised in 1804 (but the scores are lost and no one is sure what the anniversary was). There still exists a stewards notebook covering the period 1808 to 1825, and details of match scores are scattered over the next 30 odd years: the last such match took place in 1863, the year before the first scorebook in the possession of the club begins. There is evidence that the club was reformed in 1857 and 1878: after that date there are odd gaps in the series of minute books and scorebooks, but they arise from an occasional lack of liaison between successive secretaries and are not evidence of a breakdown in continuity.

The cricketers of Hambledon celebrated the 250th anniversary of their club last year, 2000. How far were they justified in doing so? The Hambledon club continued in the 1790s after the noblemen had moved their sphere of interest and their players and grand matches to London: local gentry paid local cricketers to take part in matches using the pitch and club house on Windmill Down. Arthur Haygarth confirms this at page 188 of volume 1 of Scores and Biographies. Further, in the stewards notebook there are items relating to capital expenditure, such as refurbishing the club house and mending the access way. They are by no means the initial entries in the book, which confirms that the activity recorded in 1808 was merely part of a continuing process.

The cricket played by Hambledon between 1826 and 1863, details of the players and the ground they played on are all surveyed later in this book. Even if the cricket was not continuous, it has not been difficult to find evidence of matches and there may be others, which have yet to be discovered. The reader may well conclude that there is evidence of more or less continuous activity on the cricket field in Hambledon from at least 1750 to date.

Behind the cricket, indeed behind Windmill Down, lies the village of Hambledon, the picturesque home of successive generations of cricketers who are the chief participants in this history. They may not be inhabitants of a cradle of cricket, but they have supported a long lasting and flourishing nursery.

Neil Jenkinson
January 2001

CHAPTER 1

Hambledon

You could easily miss the heart of Hambledon in Hampshire as you drive north from Waterlooville towards the Meon Valley and Winchester. After passing through the vastly expanded village of Denmead, the road narrows and curves downward for a mile or so before reaching the first scattered houses. As habitation develops on either side, the road bears left at a y-junction and, as Green Lane, runs for a mile or so past sporadic housing before climbing over the downs towards Brockbridge, the site of Droxford station, defunct since the 1950s: but Green Lane was a mere track before the coming of the railway in 1903 turned it into the main road. Until then the major highway swung right at the junction opposite The Green Man, where it becomes West Street, Hambledon and continues in a north easterly direction through the centre of the village where, at the left hand turning to High Street and the church, it becomes East Street. Hambledon lies in a side valley which runs in a north easterly direction and is so narrow that the gardens of the houses on each side run steeply up from the village street, and the view from Speltham Hill, which you reach by turning right by the George gives, as a famous visitor once wrote, a touch of Clovelly. There are a few shops - fewer than there used to be - serving the close packed cottages and more far flung houses of varying ages and styles which make up the village. There is a larger number of handsome mansions than you might expect in a place of this size, and there are some handsome gardens: this is in its own right an attractive and ancient place in which to spend an hour or two. In the XVIII and XIX Centuries it was often known as Hambledon town, and within the period since the 1st World War its shopping centre has at different times included a couple of dozen shops and businesses including those of chemist, bank, two grocers, dentist, cycle shop, butchers, tailors, ironmongers, builders, carriers, four pubs, a brewery, baker, miller, blacksmith, wheelwright, electrician, plumber and Messrs Hartridges soft drinks factory, which must be the largest and longest standing establishment of all. Until not long ago South Down buses had a depot there. At one time the village possessed an employment exchange and an accountants office: it still boasts a fine primary school on the hill between the church and Windmill Down.

Only one pub, The New Inn, remains, for The Vine Inn closed this summer: there is also a tea room to offer hospitality, but The George Hotel, formerly The George Inn, and once the home of Richard Nyren has been converted into accommodation units, and The Bat and Ball on Broadhalfpenny Down where Nyren ran the Hambledon cricket lies, not in the village, but in Clanfield parish a mile and a half up the road which is a continuation of East Street. The parish boundary in fact runs through the front bar of the pub.

Windmill Down, another ground of the XVIII Century club lies to the north of the magnificent parish church at the top of High Street and the Hambledon cricket club's own ground Ridge Meadow lies north of that in Brook Lane. The South Downs extend to the north and the west, and to east and south fold steeper wooded hills, in Hampshire called hangers.

Hambledon still seems remote when approached from any direction except Denmead. Up on Broadhalfpenny Down opposite The Bat and Ball stands the monument erected in 1908, upon which is this inscription:

> This stone marks the site
> of the ground
> of the
> Hambledon Cricket Club
> Circ 1750-1787

The dates were really invented for the monument, while the club was simply The Hambledon Club, the members having other pursuits in addition to cricket. The inn itself with its little front bar well preserved inside and out is itself also a memorial to those XVIII Century cricketers.

Thanks to modern research their matches have been identified in a series running from 1756 to 1792. After that date many of the players still engaged in big matches, but under team names other than Hambledon; only that match of 1804 may possibly have been a last great match.

The present Hambledon Cricket Club players view the year, 2000, as marking the 250th anniversary of the foundation of their club, which they have celebrated in grand style with a cricket week, a match against MCC, and the issue of a millennium souvenir and anniversary programme. The club is a successful one, and runs three Saturday league sides, a Sunday team, and participates in no fewer than three other competitions, while they have a ladies side and colts teams, all with full fixture lists.

This millennium year also sees a very happy conjunction between the Marylebone and Hambledon Cricket Clubs: for the first time ever, they will share their President. Lord Alexander of Weedon QC, the distinguished lawyer and banker, who has already been President of Hambledon for four years, takes over at the head of the affairs of MCC in October 2000, and so will bring together under his leadership the two clubs which have in succession been the guardians of the laws and standards of cricket since the mid XVIII Century. In 1787 Hambledon's grand backers moved their patronage from Hampshire to Marylebone, and central power in cricket went with them to the club which became MCC and played on the succession of grounds which became known as Lords.

Hambledon is often still and inaccurately, called The Cradle Of Cricket. In truth the origins of the game are shrouded in mystery but it had its beginnings in the Weald of Kent and East Sussex, whence it spread. Hambledon cricket could not have gained the fame it did without having equally, or almost equally, illustrious opponents to play them. All the visiting sides in the Hambledon cricket week this year are the offspring of those early rivals, Dartford, Slindon, Chertsey, Caterham, Farnham and Sevenoaks Vine.

The reason for Hambledon's pre-eminence lies in the writing, or conversation, of one man, John Nyren, whose "The Cricketers Of My Time" edited by Charles Cowden Clarke was published in book form in 1833, 40 years after the great days ended, and immortalised those forgotten cricketers, most of them by then dead. Had Nyren chronicled Dartford or Sevenoaks Vine, both of whom boast ancient cricket grounds and long histories, they might have gained the glory, but thanks to Nyren, it is the name of Hambledon which is known the world over as the place where cricket came of age.

Who can wonder at that, reading Nyren's lyrical enthusiasm about the cricket on Broadhalfpenny Down: "There would this company, consisting most likely of some thousands, remain patiently and anxiously watching every turn of fate in the game, as if the event had been the meeting of two armies to decide their liberty. And whenever a Hambledon man made a good hit, worth four or five runs, you would hear the deep mouths of the whole multitude baying away in pure Hampshire - "Go hard! - go hard! - *Tich* and turn! - *tich* and turn!"

How strongly are all those scenes, of fifty years bygone, painted in my memory! - and the smell of that ale comes upon me as freshly as the new May flowers."

The bat used on Broadhalfpenny Down, in the XVIII century. Presented to Hambledon Cricket Club by E. Whalley-Tooker. The bat is on loan to the museum at Lord's.

CHAPTER 2:
Foundations

There is no direct evidence of the foundation of the Hambledon club in the year 1750, but there are a number of indicators pointing to a date around that time or even earlier. James Pycroft was a XIX Century cricket historian and William Beldham was the finest batsman of his time, which in cricketing terms ran from 1787 to 1820, and he lived to be 96 years old at his death in 1862. He had played for the old Hambledon club and told Pycroft when they met in 1837 "If you want to know the time the Hambledon club was formed, I can tell you by this - when we beat them in 1780, I heard Mr. Powlett say "Here have I been 30 years raising our club, and are we to be beaten by a mere parish?"" But in 1780 Beldham was only 14, and the old man's memory must have been shaky. Perhaps he was five years adrift, as he is said to have played for Farnham against Hambledon in 1785 although there is no surviving record of the match. Powlett involved himself closely in the running of the club for many years. If Beldham heard Powlett's comments in that year, that would give a starting date of 1755.

An early XIX Century secretary of the Hambledon club, Thomas Smith, wrote a letter which claims an earlier date for the foundation of the club, placing it at the beginning of the XVIII Century. This text, quoted by both Pycroft in The Cricket Field (1851) and by Arthur Haygarth in Scores and Biographies, Volume 1, published in 1862, is invaluable for the later history of the club (see Chapter Three of this book), but Tom Smith was born in 1790, and his views on events before 1800 are not based on first hand knowledge and any evidence upon which he may have relied in the old books of the club is now lost. The best evidence for the foundation of the club comes from the fact that in 1756 its team was good enough to play against one of the strongest teams of the day, Dartford, not just once but twice in 10 days. The documentary evidence for the first match comes from an advertisement in the Oxford Gazette and Reading Mercury in which a clergyman from Chalton, near Petersfield, offered a reward for the return of his spaniel Rover, lost at "The cricket match on Broadhalfpenny on Wednesday 18 August 1756". The paper clearly had a wide circulation as it was published 50 miles away from Hambledon (but other issues contain several references to cricket in Hampshire relating, for example, to Eversley and Odiham) and while it raises more questions than it answers (why advertise anywhere other than in a local paper with circulation limited to Petersfield or Portsmouth? Answer: there were none) the advert does imply the presence at the match of a sufficiently large crowd for the animal to go astray and suggests a wide geographical area of interest in the play on Broadhalfpenny Down. It is the only evidence that the match took place at all. The same teams met again 10 days later at the Artillery Ground, Finsbury Square, one of the major cricketing centres of the time. Hambledon's participation at such a venue and against such opponents, suggests that the club had become an established and successful part of the cricket scene by 1756. Tradition ascribes the date of the bat at Winchester College to 1743.

By the year 1771, as Ashley Mote points out in "The Glory Days Of Cricket", Hambledon was such a force in the world of cricket that the club had authority to regulate the laws of the game. Such influence would not be granted to a fly by night organisation and to claim an origin going back to 1750 seems perfectly reasonable. This authority was derived from both the status of its principle patrons among them, latterly, the Duke of Dorset and the Earl of Winchilsea, and the playing success of the side of which there is plentiful evidence for the period 1767 to 1792.

It has long been a matter for wonder for historians that the isolated township of Hambledon and the even more remote cricket ground at Broadhalfpenny Down should have been chosen as a centre of big cricket (even if it was a cosy location for a drinking club), and that the vast crowds described by John Nyren should have made long journeys over rough tracks to see the cricket. It eventually became a matter for wonder for the club's own patrons, too, and in 1782 they opened a new ground on Windmill Down, north west of the village, and there, for the most part, they played their home matches for the remainder of the club's great days.

In 1787 Winchilsea and other aristocratic patrons of the game who were members of the White Conduit Club in London, encouraged a member of its staff called Thomas Lord to lay out a new cricket ground where they could, if they wished, disport themselves away from the vulgar gaze of the public. This he did on a site where Dorset Square was later built near what is now Marylebone Station. Winchilsea and others formed a new club to use it. So the Marylebone Cricket Club came into being. The fact that Winchilsea was President of the Hambledon club that year had absolutely no effect on that decision.

William (Silver Billy) Beldham in old age, from a painting by A. Vincent, about 1860. (By courtesy of M.C.C.)

Then in 1791 Richard Nyren, described by his son John as "the head and right arm of the club" left Hambledon, and in the following year the flow of grand cricket matches dried up.

The members of the Hambledon club were mostly backers, diners and gamblers, as opposed to players, and their meetings were able to continue into 1796. Membership declined, and with the outbreak of the war with France, which caused fear of invasion, and members to enlist in the colours or to retreat to supposed safety inland, the days of the club were numbered. There is something very strange about the last meetings: the one held on 29 August 1796 attracted only three members but they brought with them the large number of twelve non subscribers who included, to quote from the minutes "Mr. Tho Pain Authour of the rights of man". The minute adds "no business noted." It was a sensational event for Paine to be in England at all at that time, let alone in the company of 14 true-bred Englishmen. The publication of his book "The Rights Of Man" resulted in his having to flee the country to avoid prosecution for sedition and he had only recently been released from prison in France, yet no one who had been at that meeting grassed on him. If the club in its isolated decline was a hot bed of treasonable extreme left wing activity, there is no evidence at all to confirm it, although Henry Bonham, the club secretary, was well known locally as a radical, which in official circles was a term of abuse. We do not even know whose guest Paine was.

So to the next, and final meeting recorded in the minutes:

Sepr 21st - No Gentlemen.

But there were still a few in the neighbourhood.

Chapter Three
On Windmill Down

A booklet issued in 1908 to commemorate the first important match on Broadhalfpenny Down since 1792 describes how the Hambledon Club was reconstituted in May 1800, the President being Admiral Hamilton of Hill House, and the Vice President Thomas Butler. There are lingering traces of activity after 1796 for on 27 April 1799, the Earl of Winchilsea paid for his dinner and subscription to the "Cricket Club" which E.E. Snow identified as the Hambledon Club in the Journal of the Cricket Society, Autumn 1976 page 26, and Spring 1977 page 5. The Earl's accounts also display a gentleman's love of gambling: between June and September 1792, his Lordship records gambling winnings of £229.8.0 (£229.40p) that is in modern terms £25,000.

Norman Gannaway refers to a game, East Meon and Stoke versus Hambledon in 1801, and there was comment on the later years of this Club in mid Victorian times. Volume One of Arthur Haygarth's Scores and Biographies recalled that "An old style bat was hung over the dining table in the club house on Windmill Down (where the club first played in 1782) until the year 1819 when a member of the club after dinner by way of frolic took it down and insisted on having one hit with it.... it fell all to pieces....the club was very well kept up until about 1825 when many members left the neighbourhood, the old club house having fallen into decay and Windmill Down was ploughed up shortly after."

Haygarth ends on a note of hope with the expectation in 1857 that the club may again be established on a new ground offered by a descendant of an old patron of the noble game, Mr. Foster.

John Foster (1803-1858) inherited Park House on the death in 1846 of his father, also John, to whom it passed on the death of his uncle Mr. Land in 1791. John Foster Junior was a benefactor of the cricket club as we shall see. His family were involved with it during the later period of its activity, touched on by Haygarth as can be seen from a notebook deposited in the Hampshire Record Office following its discovery in a bricked up bread oven in a cottage in the village. This leather bound volume provides details of the club's activity between 1808 and 1825. It does not carry the name of the Hambledon Club but its references to "the Down", and the names of Bonham, Hale, Hamilton, Butler and Ridge, which are well known from the

Park House, Hambledon, home of John Foster to whom Hambledon's present ground was alloted under the Inclosure Acts in 1857.

earlier days of the club, clearly confirm the connection. It is the steward's notebook, containing his references to the purchase of the implements of the game and to feasting on the Down and it confirms many details of the existence of the club up to 1825. The first entry is dated 2 May 1808, which is 11 or so years after the famous last entry in the minute book.

J. Stewart signed the initial entries which were subsequently made up by A. Laurence. They show the names of the players in each match who are carefully distinguished between gentlemen, whose names are prefixed "Mr" or with their rank or title and the bare surnames of the players. There is a note of the amount paid to each of these for each match and the notes almost always include a reference to the pay of the umpire and scorer.

As in the published accounts of the great days, the steward, who received a guinea a session (£1.05p) as a minimum, carefully noted the number of diners: the largest party of those who remained to eat dinner was seven, but the expressions "no members present" and indeed "no gentlemen" recur.

The subscribers for 1811 were W. Bonham, W. Hale, Captain Halcott, W.A. Hamilton, W. Goodlad, Admiral Hamilton, Col C. Todd, Captain Douglas, W.M. Purdey, W. Bailey, Sir Thomas Champness, W. Butler, Lt. Col Cuppage, Rev G. Richards, Col C. King, Rev W. Garnier, R. Griffinhoofe, Captain E.J. Ridge, and Rev Hill.

Five of these, as already noted, had been subscribers to the club in the previous century, as recorded in F.S. Ashley Cooper's "The Hambledon Cricket Chronicle". Butler is one of the family who moved to Hambledon in 1800 and whose members often played in the games on Windmill Down in the 1800s. Apart from them not one of these subscribers is noted as a player in the stewards book. Of the others Griffinhoofe is the name of a firm of solicitors in London and Champness was associated with a school in Winchester, Hyde Abbey House, whose headmaster in the early XIX century was the son of Reynell Cotton, the composer of the Hambledon Club cricket song. Col Todd was actively involved in running the club, as the steward notes on many occasions that he helped reconcile the accounts. Henry Bonham and his brother Thomas were in turn the honorary secretaries of the club in the 1790s, but neither of them left any children and I can find no indication as to what their relationship was to W. Bonham. A cousin of the Bonhams, John Carter inherited Thomas's Estate in 1826 and added Bonham to his surname.

W. Hale's family owned Windmill Down, and lived at Hambledon House near the George Inn. The Goodlad family lived at Hill Place, Bishops Waltham.

Hamilton/Admiral Hamilton. Neither Sir Charles Hamilton nor his brother Sir Edward achieved flag rank until after 1814 and both are too young to be the Captain Hamilton who became a member of the club in 1783 and was President in 1800. King may be related to John King of Corhampton who was master of the Hambledon Hounds from 1829 to 1841. Ridge. T. J. Ridge was a banker living in Hambledon itself.

A name frequently mentioned in the steward's book is that of the Secretary Thomas Smith, who is not to be confused with Thomas Assheton Smith, who, like him, was a celebrated horseman as well as being a competent cricketer but was also MP for Andover. Our Tom Smith, lived at Hill House, Hambledon during his period in office. It is from his letter that Pycroft quoted at great length in the Cricket Field about the later years of the club, which Haygarth also used in Volume One of Scores and Biographies; and to which I have referred at the beginning of this chapter.

The anonymous author of Smith's biography "The Life Of Another Tom Smith" refers to Butler and Richards as constantly in attendance at the club's matches, adding that the old Club was in full swing when Smith took over as secretary and organised the matches, "and from

An extract from the steward's notebook.

the old club books which came into his hands we glean some curious particulars." It is a big let down that he supplies no details but he does tell us that Smith usually prevailed on William Ward, the banker, MP and holder of the record individual score, 280, to attend these Hambledon matches.

There are famous names among the players too, like Lear, Newland, Aylward and Aburrow, which echo past glories, while others provide a link with the future of the club: Baigley [Beagley?], Foster again, Bulbeck, Poole, Jerram, Edney, Meredith and Abinett.

A typical entry at the end of 1812 reads:

after balance with Col Todd for the year 1812, I paid the expenses of the Winchester match, ... £1.6.3d (£1.32p), and umpire and scorer £1 each. .... £32.17.6d (£32.81p) Recd of Mr. Richards on Mr. Rashleigh's account, after balance with Col Todd £6.6.0d (£6.30p)

Then
<u>Expenses for 1813</u>
Menden the Down and cutting the turf £0.10.6
Rowling the Down £0.12.0
Small's bill £1.19.6
Set stumps £0.10.6
Forgat (sic)
Advertising the anniversary £0.7.0
Punch for the anniversary £2.2.0
New ball £0.6.0
Set of stumps £0.10.6
<u>Expenses for 1814</u>
November 4 [1813] cutting turf/layen carridge £0.16.0
April 22 rowlen the Down £0.10.6
Advertising the anniversary £0.7.0
Advertising printing the meetings £0.7.0
[??] the thatching £0.2.0
Small's bill: 5 bats and 2 balls £1.13.0
Set stumps £0.10.6
Garrett bill £0.5.0
<u>Expenses for 1815</u>
Cutting turf for repairing the Down £0.8.0
Paid thatcher for straw £0.3.6
[Broadhalfpenny?] Down £0.10.6
Give the plays for punch £1.1.6
Batt of Garrett £0.4.0
Small: bill £1.7.6
Mr. Sueter: bill £0.7.3
Tobacco and pipes £0.10.6
Given the players punch £1.1.0
[?] subscriptions £1.0.0
May 1 anniversary. Present
Revd Mr. Richards
Dr. Hale
Capt Bligh
Mr. Haster.

Capt Bligh is definitely not William Bligh of the Bounty who was promoted as a Vice Admiral of the Blue in 1814 by which year he was aged 60.

The steward names only three of Hambledon's opponents, Winchester in 1812 and 1821, Portsmouth 1815, and Goodwood 1824 but Norman Gannaway records that in 1806 Hambledon "fetched 144" against Winchester and that they played Goodwood in 1818 while in "Pre-Victorian Sussex Cricket", H.F. and A.P. Squire refer to two matches in 1824 both in August against Goodwood and spread over two days and as we shall see at the beginning of the next chapter Squire and Norman Gannaway refer to other matches.

In summary, the club seems to have prospered up to the end of the Napoleonic wars in mid 1815. After that season, a page has been cut out of the steward's book and the story does not pick up until 3 May 1819. The gap spanning 3 seasons may be symptomatic of a decline in activity and the subscribers named at that time in the book may represent new management. Those whose names are given for the first time are Poulter, possibly the parson at Meonstoke, named by William Cobbett in Rural Rides, Gage, Worsley, Kelsall, Boyle, Dickenson and Goruchi, but Smith, Richards and Butler maintain their lengthy connection with the club.

On 2 and 16 August 1819 more than 22 people turned up to play and the steward noted

> *Received the whole of Mr. Smith* £27.3.9
> *Game license* £3.14.6
> £30.18.3

In 1820 the club spent sums on the Windmill Down house, purchasing straw and rods, timber, the services of the sawyer, *nailes* and *poles for punchens*. The last item defeats me but it did not come very expensive as the total sum was only £2.10.0 (£2.50).

By this time the cost of a new cricket ball was seven shillings (35p). There had probably been a club house on the Down since 1783 and there was certainly a lodge there a year later when there are references in the club minutes to the hanging of a bell and making alterations including erection of a *dulce lenimen* for the ladies and later a convenience for the steward too. The most significant reference comes in the Hampshire Directory for 1793 where Ronald Knight records "on Windmill Down is a new building for the selected gentlemen of the cricketing club to dine and enjoy their beverages in, which assembly annually meets in May and continues weekly every Monday till the season for partridge shooting commences."

The exact position of both ground and building is uncertain. Was the ground to the East of the summit where it would overlook the mansion Whitedale or did it lie further West with a prospect towards the Meon valley? An aerial survey failed to reveal any trace of a clue and the large-scale map prepared in 1842 in connection with Tithe apportionment, by which time Edward Hale was both owner and occupier shows no building and makes no reference to the ground at all.

I brought a year of frustrated enquiry to an end at Portsmouth Central Library when in a drawer of XVIII Century maps I found one published by W. Faden in 1791 following a survey by T. Milner which clearly showed the Cricket House on the summit of Windmill Down to the rear of Whitedale; better still a map brought out in April 1810 by Lt-Col Mudge at the Tower of London delineates the "Cricketers Down" as a specific enclosure approached by what appears to be a track running from East Street on the North side of Whitedale. The stewards book notes the expense of *layen carridge*, which is a reference to the access track. There is still a driveway to the North of Whitedale, which now terminates by the vineyard. The other access to Windmill Down from the village runs North West from the primary school, but as this is now no more than a narrow footpath running through the crops it seems probable that the drive from East Street was the way the cricketers reached Windmill Down.

The cricketers worked hard on the ground again in 1821, when 300 turf were cut (at seven and a half pence a hundred) and laid over three days! Boards, nails, locks and *matts* were all replaced and the club hired a horse which was kept on the Down. As late as 1824, as already noted two games of two days duration were played against Goodwood and a week later the club was able to place two elevens which played each other on the Down but from this point decline soon followed and that was the club's last full season. The following season did not start until 13 June and there was no cricket between 20 June and 11 July when as many as seven gentlemen and 13 paid players took part and there were 18 including five gentlemen on 25 July. As a last reckoning, on 1 August the participants were Mr. T. Butler, Mr. C. Butler, Mr. Cotman, Mr. Gauntlet with Stewart, Littlefield, Knight and Colles forming one team and Mr. Foster, Mr. S. Butler, Capt Georges with Jarman, Kelsey, Langtree and Littlefield making up the

W. Faden's map of 1791 showing the Cricket House on Windmill Down

opposition. However for August 8, 15, 22, 29, the entries all have a familiar ring

No meetings

Mr. Stewart recorded the collection of subscriptions simultaneously for the seasons of 1823, 1824 and 1825, totalling £19.80, as if in a final attempt to settle up, and there are no subsequent entries in the book. There may of course have been other records which are now missing - it is after all pure chance that this notebook came to light. Alternatively after 1825 sides were raised by Hambledon only on an Ad Hoc basis, but as a result of the researches by Squire, it is reasonable to conclude that Windmill Down supported the game up to 1836.

Why did the club suffer a decline in the 1820s? In that decade the economy of the country faltered; there were many fluctuations in the value of the pound and a disastrous deterioration in the state of agriculture. As to Hambledon itself, William Cobbett paints a pathetic picture in Rural Rides after a visit in 1822 indicating that it must once have been a considerable place boasting a church pretty nearly as large as that at Farnham in Surrey which is quite sufficient for a large town. The rent of houses had fallen from £40 or £50 a year to 3 or 4 shillings (15-25p) a week and even at those rents thousands could not be let at all to anybody capable of paying rent.

In October 1826 he visited his old Hambledon friend Mr. Goldsmith at West End about a mile from the village where he writes "it was formerly a considerable market town and it had three fairs in the year. There is now not even the name of market left and the fairs amount to little more than a couple or three ginger bread stalls, with dolls and whistles for children."

The decline in prosperity, coupled with the mechanisation of agriculture lead to widespread unrest in the countryside resulting in some places in damage to crops and machinery, and rioting. Perhaps it is surprising that this isolated club lasted as long as it did.

The Down was woodland by the 1880s. Now it is open and arable with a fairly new plantation of spruce on the Northern slope. The summit is divided by a hedge, the soil is stony and there is nothing to suggest that this was for over 50 years a well developed home of cricket. From the summit long views of down and woodland extend to East and North. To the South Hambledon is concealed in its narrow valley. It is almost impossible to imagine the bustle and enjoyment on the Down 180 years ago when as Tom Smith's biographer wrote "the place was always a scene of gaiety on such occasions as it was Mr. Smith's custom to invite all the strangers to his house and the evening was usually finished up with a dance."

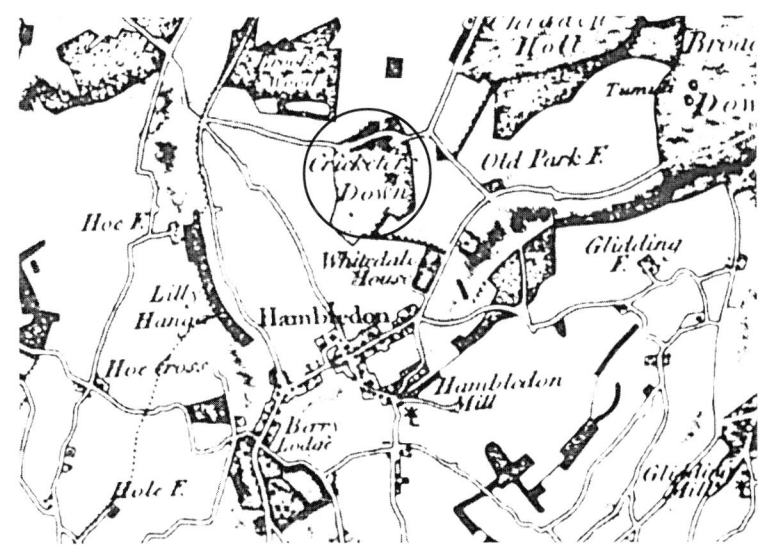

Map published 10 April 1810 by Colonel Mudge showing the Cricket Down at the rear of Whitedale, Hambledon.

An extract from the Club's first scorebook, 1864.

Chapter 4
Brook Lane

In later years Squire has found two Hambledon matches with Midhurst in 1829, two in 1835 home and away with Goodwood, and three in August 1836 when Hambledon's opponents were again Goodwood. Three of these matches are described as played on Windmill Down, including the last one, which was played on 22 August 1836, 11 years after the stewards last entries, and post-dating by 17 years the year when the clubhouse is said to have been tumbledown. Further, Norman Gannaway records a Hambledon victory over Newport, presumably on the Island, in 1834 when the Hambledon team was T. Bulbeck, Foster, Pay, Hammond, Boyce, Friend, Etherington, Gale, Bligh, Downman and Garrett.

On 24 June 1844 the South Hants Cricket Club met Hambledon at Daniel Day's ground at Itchen, Southampton - and beat them. A year later they drew at the same venue but between their two sorties to Southampton, Hambledon offered a return match at home. Where did they play? Both Broadhalfpenny and Windmill Downs had returned to agriculture so one looks for a third ground, perhaps one carved out for the occasion in the valley to the right of the road opposite Fairfield or Whitedale, or possibly at Bury Lodge where one game is recorded in 1869. This may have been at Chestnut Meadow, the ground of the former Hambledon Football Club, on the opposite side of the Denmead road from Bury Lodge. As there is no local tradition to support play opposite Fairfield or Whitedale, it is tempting to allocate this match to the club's present ground, Ridge Meadow, in Brook Lane, whose use for recreation was recognised when the field was inclosed in 1857, and again in 1861. Why should a recreational use be assigned to Brook Lane in a document as formal as an inclosure award under Act of Parliament, if there was not already a tradition of play there? But there is no positive indication of any cricket being played there between 1836 and 1857, the year when Hambledon undoubtedly did play at Brook Lane.

There are other pointers to continuity of play in Hambledon: the names of the same players recur. The team which played South Hants on 9 September 1845 included Bulbeck, the surgeon, Meredith, Pink, Gamman or Gaman, Greentree and Higgens. The first two names appear in the steward's notebook and Bulbeck as well as Foster played against Newport in 1834 while the names of Gaman, Greentree, Higgens, Foster and Pink figure in the matches recorded in the earliest scorebook in 1864. Of course the names may refer to successive generations of cricketers rather than the same individuals. A further indication of play at Brook Lane itself comes from a note, which appears to have been inserted in 1920, at the beginning of that first scorebook, that cricket had been played there from 1855.

Fred Gale, the XIX century Wykehamist and journalist records in *The Game of Cricket* published in 1887 that "there was a match every Sunday afternoon until the ground was enclosed, and possibly this may have been fatal to the continuance of the cricket ground..." and a few pages later "the ground in front of the old Bat and Ball was enclosed and the land was exchanged for some other land near the village, because the Sunday cricket matches were played there till about 30 years ago, which fact occasioned the exchange."

These passages suggest that Broadhalfpenny Down saw play until the 1850s, but there is no evidence of this at all and the information available supports Windmill Down as the ground where play went on well through the XIX century. There was undoubtedly an exchange of land under the Inclosure Acts in 1861 but neither Broadhalfpenny Down nor Windmill Down was involved, and as Ashley Mote has shown it was Brook Lane which was allotted to John Foster "To be held by him and his heirs subject to an obligation to preserve the surface in good condition and permitting such land to be at all times used as a place of exercise and recreation for the inhabitants of the said village and neighbourhood."

The importance of what Fred Gale wrote after his visit to Hambledon (which was in 1879) was his reference to the playing of cricket *in the village* 30 years earlier.

In 1897 E.V. Lucas, the essayist and critic described how the summit of Windmill Down was divided between rank grass and a copse of fir trees and larches. He continues "early in our (XIX) century the ground was once more changed to its present site... the turf of the present ground, which you reach by descending Windmill Down and climbing a mere mound which lies to the North of it, is the same turf on which Beldham batted and Harris bowled."

So there is a tradition of continuity of play at Hambledon and there is nothing to suggest that any ground other than the three famous venues was used.

CHAPTER 5

Recorded History

Haygarth's prophesy was fulfilled. The inclosure award in favour of John Foster was dated 14 January 1857. The earliest entry in the club's next surviving records is the minute of a meeting "of the members of the Hambledon Cricket Club" held at the New Inn on 21 April 1857 which records a resolution that Jno Foster Esq be appointed President and Captain Jessop Vice President and names as committee for that year John Goldsmith, M.L. Caley, D. Lunn, R. Pink, G. Pink, E. Boardman, J. Gaman, Jno Foster Snr, Wm Friend and Captain Jessop. Gaman was elected Treasurer and Sidney Lunn Secretary. The club purchased six match balls from Lillywhites for the sum of £2.5.0 (£2.25), a set of practice stumps for five shillings (25p) and leg guards and wicket keeping gloves. The club held a monthly dinner day but the actual matches were few in number: there was a practice game on 4 June and later in the month they played a home fixture with Fareham and they also played Petersfield at home on 10 July with a return match on 11 August. The fifth game was with Portsdown. None of the scores has survived.

Sidney Lunn noted the names of 48 members for that season and those who played a significant part in the club's history included:-

T. Ridge. One of the local gentry whose family connections with the club went back to the XVIII Century.

T. Butler. The father of Thomas Butler the future President of the club.

Revd T. Patteson. The long serving vicar of Hambledon (1841-1874).

George Pink. A maltster and timber surveyor.

R. Pink. Land surveyor and insurance agent.

E. Hale. One of the family who were the owners of Windmill Down and also took part in the matches there.

George Greentree. A butcher in the village: a relative, John, kept the Green Man.

H. Jarman. A Mrs Jarman farmed near Hambledon at Chidden.

John Bulbeck. Surgeon.

James Batts. A bricklayer.

George Beagley. A relation of Thomas Beagley, the famous batsman of the first half of the XIX Century. Marion Beagley and her brother

Robert, respectively Secretary and Chairman of Hambledon Cricket Club are of the same family.

W. Langrish. Players of this name represented the club over a period of 75 years.

W.H. Barkworth. One of the local gentry who lived at Cams Cottage.

M.L. Caley. A builder, wheelwright and carpenter.

Henry Rosier. Landlord of The New Inn.

G.H. Jones of Ashling House, medical practitioner.

The next meeting of the club was held on 29 March 1858 when J.J. Higgens was elected President (John Foster Snr died during the year) and John Goldsmith was elected Vice President. The season was to open on the first Thursday in May with a practice match, at which dinner was taken on the ground at 3pm. The number of members who signed up that year reduced to 25 and we have the scores of only two matches both against Petersfield who were successful each time. Gaman however took 12 wickets in the two matches, in the later of which Hambledon made their opponents task much easier by conceding 23 wides.

Only one match is recorded in 1859, a rather featureless draw against Winchester Garrison and the number of subscribers reduced to 20. The accounts for that year allow glimpses of the teams play. There was expenditure in connection with the Petersfield match on 11 June which included payment for the umpire and two of the players, Dilloway and Langrish and dinner for presumably the same two as well as the scorer. The next game noted was the return at home nearly five weeks later and a week after that T. Clay received one shilling (5p) for mowing the ground in preparation for the match with Purbrook. The only other fixture that season was the return with Purbrook.

The club funds at the end of the 1859 season, £3.6.10 were then carried forward to the year 1862 when the only recorded activity was home and away matches with Wickham, which suggest that the two intervening seasons were fallow. It is cheering to find increased activity in 1863 and much more in the season after that. Gear was purchased from both Clapshaw's and Lillywhites and the club paid George Greentree for making a frame for marking the creases: an interesting innovation at a time when creases had customarily been cut into the turf rather than marked with whitewash. Hambledon played two games with the Fourth Brigade RA based at Hillsea, one of them recorded in Haygarth's Scores and Biographies, Volume page 165. The score is

CHAPTER 5

...page 33. The last recorded match, on 26 August, was against ...n. Although it is called the return match there is no note of ...s of an earlier match. One of these games may be the one in ...e scoring was so low that Sidney Lunn contemplated sending ...s to the Sporting Journal, Bells Life in London. Hambledon ...es of 33 and 36 turned out as winners against Horndean with ...3. John Gaman was topscorer in the match with nine in the ...ings: E. Tandy had 12 victims and F. Jackman six for ...lon.

... the club played a much fuller season, including trips to ...ville, Gosport and Hillsea. Mr. Rosier provided the transport ...; 13 shillings and sixpence (68p) for a pair of horses to ...ville and back, a wagonette to Gosport and back was 15 ...and a pair of horses, Hillsea return, was £1.2.6.

...el on the front of the club's first surviving scorebook reads ...don Cricket Club 1864". Inside the front cover there is a note ...ok was kept by Sidney Lunn who was secretary of the club ...e whole of the time. It is believed that there had been no ...ny stress) cricket club in the parish before this for very many ...B. The matches were all whole day. The present (1920) cricket ...as made about 1855."

...year 1864 was a highly significant one in terms of the ...ent of cricket, for Sidney Lunn to open his new scorebook. ...ring, George Parr brought his English touring side safely ...n its visit to Australia, the second such trip down under; there ...of a formation of a cricket parliament to develop the game ...ce the laws of cricket; a professional travelling XI, the United ...England XI, joined a number of similar touring sides which ...advantage of improved railway facilities to spread quality ...all corners of the country: both Middlesex and Lancashire ...Cricket Clubs were formed, and John Wisden, one of the ...bowlers of his time gave his name to his first almanac. The ...so saw the initial appearances in good cricket of the 16-year-...Grace, although his first class entry did not take place until ...ving year.

...from all these events, the one with the greatest long-term ...s something different: the recognition that overarm bowling ...e to stay. The middle XIX Century was full of cricket ...rsies over issues which are totally dead today; round arm ...that is delivering the ball with the arm no higher than the

ERRATUM

Page 10, line 1 should read "Only one pub, The Vine Inn, remains, for The New Inn closed last summer":

– 31 –

shoulder, had been legalised in 1833 after years of dispute yet within 20 years some bowlers were wanting to go one better and bowl with the arm higher than the shoulder, indeed brushing the ear. Edgar Willsher of Kent a fine professional medium pace bowler was one of the leaders of the movement, and on a famous occasion at the Oval in 1862 was no balled although most umpires up to then had overlooked the height of his delivery. Some observers thought that that event was a put up job which was intended to bring matters literally to a head. If that was so, the manoeuvre proved effective as on 10 June 1864 MCC legalised overarm bowling.

The changes in the law did not mean that bowlers immediately abandoned their existing under arm, or round arm styles: those who achieved success by bowling under arm continued to bowl it until age and retirement diminished their numbers. Even in first class cricket at least one lob bowler survived until 1921. Similarly round arm bowlers who were successful with that delivery continued until they had bowled themselves into retirement. Those who had already, and illegally adopted the overarm style of course continued with it and as new generations came to play the game they followed the latest fashion.

So a spectator of Hambledon in their games in 1864 would have seen bowling mostly in the round arm style which had been legal for 30 years with perhaps the odd lobster entering the attack and a number of practitioners of the new fangled overarm: a real mix. Each bowler would have to inform the batsman which style he was going to use before he bowled.

These developments were deeply unpopular in some quarters. To John Nyren writing in the 1830s anything other than under arm bowling constituted throwing.

Local legend has it that when the Hambledon Club went to play at Windmill Down they took their turf with them and years later they again carefully removed it to Brook Lane. This deserves to be true, but overlooks the fact that the club played on BOTH of the earlier grounds between 1782 and 1792. More likely is the version given by Ashley Mote, that a group of the cricket club members carefully cut a swathe of rough turf from the abandoned Broadhalfpenny Down, and re-laid it at Brook Lane, 2 miles down the road.

Although the scorebook starts in 1864, there is one recorded match from the previous season (and why shouldn't there be others) in which Hambledon defeated the Fourth Brigade Royal Artillery at Hilsea by 96 runs. The scores were (but the Hambledon extras do not add up):

At HILSEA, August 13, 1863

HAMBLEDON

F. Jackman, c Spinks, b Sandover 64	— c Robson, b Sandover 19
—Tandy, c Pipon, b Robson 10	— l b w., b Sandover 18
— Greentree, c Loraine, b Sandover 9	— not out 21
C. Higgens, Esq., b Sandover 0	— c Robson, b Sandover 9
T. Butler, Esq., c Bastow, b Sandover 2	— run out 0
—Lunn, run out 2	— b Sandover 2
—Goldsmith, Esq., l b w, b—— 1	— c Robson, b Sandover 7
W. Higgens, Esq., c Pipon, b Sandover 1	— c Pipon, b Sandover 0
G. Butler, Esq., b Sandover 0	— c Martin, b Sandover 0
—Foster, not out 2	— l b w, b—— 2
—Humphrey, b Sandover 3	— b Sandover 0
Byes 6, leg byes 4, wides 9 18	Byes 0, 1 b 2, wides 6 .. 8
112	86

FOURTH BRIGADE ROYAL ARTILLLRY.

Lieut. Loraine, c T. Butler, b Jackman .. 2	— not out 2
Sergt. Spinks, b Jackman 3	— b Tandy 1
Lieut. Orange, b Jackman 0	— b Tandy 11
Capt. Downman, b Jackman 10	— c Humphrey, b Tandy 2
Sergt Sandover, b Jackman 7	— run out 0
Capt. Martin, not out 31	— c T. Butler, b Jackman 0
Col. Bastow, run out 1	— l b w, b Jackman 0
Lieut. Toogood, run out 1	— c and b Jackman 0
Lieut. Pipon, run out 11	— b Jackman 3
Lieut. Robson, b Jackman 5	— b Tandy 0
Lieut. Tupper, b Jackman 1	— b Tandy 0
Byes 6, leg bye 1, wide 1, noes 2 .. 10	Bye 1, wides 0 1
82	20

The first match recorded in the book was against Waterloo Park on Friday 3 June 1864, when the Hambledon team was J. Gaman, W. Goldsmith, F. Jackman, S. Lunn, W. Higgens, W. Humphrey T. Butler, N. Hodgson, W. Hall, J. Foster and F. Poole. Hambledon scored 65 (Foster 26) and 27 for 2: Waterloo Park who probably batted first totalled 83 and 94. Jackman took 6 wickets but his full analysis was not recorded. A week later the club played the Royal Artillery in a game typical of many undertaken over the next 75 years, in that two complete innings were played on each side in a single day, Hambledon with scores of 82 and 121 defeating the RA, 64 for 9 wickets and 47 by 92 runs. Butler scored 35 and Goldsmith 33 in the first innings and E. Greentree 28 and Jackman 20 in the second. Gaman and Jackman took all 19 wickets of the opposition. F. Meredith and F. Godrich were newcomers to the side in the third game, the return with Waterloo Park which Hambledon lost by 7 runs.

In the fourth match Hambledon, with 140, beat Gosport by 9 runs. Greatrex, Thresher and Case made their first appearances for the village, Thresher marking his debut by taking seven wickets. After losing to 11 officers of the 53rd Regiment, the club won the final three matches on the first innings thanks to Gaman and Jackman who continued to take the lions share of the wickets. The final game of the season again against the RA was notable only for the fact that the clubs total of 116 included 22 byes and 13 wides, so that the seasons record was played 8, won 1, lost 2, drawn 5 of which four were won on the first innings and 1 lost.

The scorebook is on deep blue paper. It does not record the venue or space for the bowling analysis. There were 8 recorded matches in 1865. They present an odd picture because 6 of them were played against the Royal Artillery or their officers. Some pages are missing or damaged while other games may have been spoiled by rain, but what is clear is that Hambledon defeated 11 of Hinton House (presumably Hinton Daubney, which was at that time a school run by the Revd John Lake Barton and was the ancestral home of the Whalley-Tooker family), by an innings and 78 runs. E. Goldsmith contributed 37 to the clubs 153, while Jackman took 8 wickets in the two innings of the opponents. In August J. Goldsmith scored 36 in Hambledon's second innings of 100 enabling them to beat the 52nd Regiment Portsmouth by 21 runs. Gaman, Wyndham and Higgens all bowled with success.

For 1866 only 2 games are recorded, both won by the club, against the Royal Marines and the RA. Butler and Jackman took wickets and Higgens hit up the large proportion of 39 in the match-winning total of 88 against the RA.

Then silence. There are no recorded fixtures for either of the two following seasons before there was a resurgence in 1869 when a mixed selection of 9 games was played including Col Butler's XI v. 101st Regiment of Fusiliers, Married v. Single and Hambledon Parish v. Droxford Parish.

At the start of the season, a team from Harting in West Sussex totalled 40 and 49 to lose to Hambledon, 37 and 54 for 1 by 9 wickets. Gaman captured seven Harting wickets in the first innings and Jackman five in the second.

G.H. Butler was the most successful batsman with scores of 24, 28, 62 and 21 not out, his 62 being the first recorded score over 50 for the club and the sides innings total of 183 was the highest to date. Yet Hambledon could only muster seven players against Harting in August, so small wonder they could scramble only 27 runs. Gaman and Jackman continued their good form with the ball. Team totals of three figures continued to be rare but an exception came in the match against Major Clay's XI at Catisfield, Fareham when the scratch sides total of 179 was overtaken by Hambledon with three wickets in hand and the innings ended when they reached of 222 which remained a record for very many years. T.H. Wilson's was the first century for the club, H.S. Dutton hit up 48 and E. Humphrey 24. An elegantly hand written note records "light very bad towards the end". Lucky for Major Clay! A summary at the end of the book shows 6 matches treated as official, of which an equal number were won and lost.

There are no more recorded matches until 1884 and the first available minute book does not start until 1878. Are these fragments of activity 135 years ago the matches recalled by the ruddy Hampshire man who, in 1897, told the author E.V. Lucas that when he was younger they used to play every Sunday afternoon; they played for pints? No they are not. All the matches recorded for 1864 and 1865 bar one were played on weekdays. Weekend cricket did not come in until around the turn of the century.

The side's opponents have a distinctly military caste. The families of the players at that time, if not always the individuals, can be identified and they represent a mixed bunch. Of the members of the first team given in the earliest scorebook we can say:

J. Gaman. John Gaman of Antill House was a surgeon. Robert Gaman also lived there as did his sisters who kept a small private school which continued into the 1920s.

J. Goldsmith of West End, was a farmer from a family long established in Hambledon which is represented there today by another John Goldsmith, the author of the standard history of the village.

F. Jackman is almost certainly Frederick Jackman, born 15 May 1841, at Fareham, died 1891 at Catherington, who was engaged by the club as a professional for 1882 (see page 40 post), who played for Hampshire in 1875 and 1877.

S. Lunn. There were Lunns in Hambledon in the mid XIX Century who were farmers, brewers, maltsters, spirit merchants and corn merchants. To which of these Sidney Lunn was related history does not disclose. He was secretary of the club from 1864 onwards. Ida Barrett who is still involved with the club and whose son Colin was one of its most successful players and captains of modern times had a great uncle named Lunn.

W. Higgens. There were two families of this name who lived in the Regency Country House, Fairfield, and its equally fine neighbour Whitedale in Hambledon. Very much local gentry, they were related by marriage to the Goldsmiths.

W. Humphrey. He cannot be specifically identified. A John Humphrey was the assistant overseer of Hambledon parish administering the poor law for the Hambledon division of Droxford Union. The family remained in the village until recent times.

T. Butler. We know more about Thomas Dacres Butler than anyone else from that era. He was the grandson of the Thomas Butler of Bury Lodge who was Vice President of the club from May 1800. T.D. Butler was himself President of Hambledon CC from 1879 until his death aged 92 in 1937: he was a frequent player in the early days, had a major part in pulling the club together in 1882 and was an authoritative representative of the club at the unveiling of the monument in 1908. In his early days he was a Captain in the 52nd Light Infantry, which may account for the military aspect of the teams early opponents. He was subsequently called to the bar and became secretary to the Lord Great Chamberlain and Deputy Black Rod in the House of Lords. He was knighted in 1918.

N. Hodgson. Nothing is known.

W. Hall. The first of a large number of players of that surname to play for the village over the span of 100 years.

J. Foster. Perhaps the son of John Foster who was allotted the cricket field under the Inclosure Acts and who died in 1858.

F. Poole. A member of another well known Hambledon family, shopkeepers and tradesmen well into the XX Century.

Greentree. Although not in that very first side, John Greentree was a frequent performer for the club in the early years. He was a farmer and landlord of The Green Man, now a private house opposite the junction of West Street and Green Lane. As we have seen, another member of the family, G. Greentree was a butcher.

F. Meredith. The family were builders and undertakers, which subsequently traded under the name of Banting and Meredith. The Bantings later became associated with the cricket club right up to the present day.

How would these cricketers appear to a spectator? Their pictures have not come down to us but some of their contemporaries were photographed. The celebrated practitioner Roger Fenton photographed the match between Hunsdonbury and the Royal Artillery as early as 1857 (see illustration). Some players are all in white, some have dark, and rather tight trousers, some have dark shirts and others are clad all in black. The scene with two umpires and at least eight fielders on view depicts a formal game of cricket, but it is not possible to work out whether the military team are in the field and wearing part of their uniform. The batsmen are arrayed in light trousers and dark shirts and the striker appears to be wearing a slouch hat while his partner is topped by a round "pill box" item of headgear. Several fielders wear baggy caps as do some of the Slindon players of 1863 in their team photograph (see illustration). The majority of their team wear white or light coloured trousers, but only four are dressed all in white. There are pads in evidence - one pair shared between two batsmen.

We can well believe that the Hambledon players of 1864 would have looked much like the cricketers in these photographs, waistcoats and all.

We cannot tell the colours from these magnificent old pictures but the cricket historian H.S. Altham (who comes into the story later) carried out researches from which he concluded that shirts patterned with coloured spots, stripes or checks, on a white background came in in the 1850s and that the commonly worn black shoes of that period progressively gave way to boots, either brown, or white with brown straps. White buckskin boots which served cricketers and bowlers in particular so well for 100 years were first worn around 1882, but only gradually superseded the brown and white type. You might have been seen wearing a blazer as early as the 1850s, if you were very smart but it was 20 years before they became popular. Some players wore their working clothes, as they still did as late as the 1950s.

The Slindon Players of 1863

The second document in the archive is a minute book covering the years 1878 to 1882 which coincided with a period of great expansion in cricket when the second, third and fourth tours of Australian cricketers to Great Britain took place. The minutes contain indications that the club was refounded in 1878. On Wednesday 3 July a General Meeting agreed to form a committee for the season and to have their clubhouse at The George Inn which had been Richard Nyren's hostelry for 20 years up to 1791. A. Arnold was elected as captain and four days later the committee met to form bye laws, resolved to buy cricketing gear through the Civil Service Stores and decided that the colours of the club were to be a blue cap with a white star.

The committee was A. Arnold, President, G.M. Knight, Vice President, W. Walter, Treasurer, and J.A. Best Hon Secretary, together with I. Hunt, G. Royle, A. Whittenham, G. Beagley, W. Humphrey, W. Lang and H. Meredith. There were changes in 1879 when Captain T.D. Butler began his 58-year stint as President on the proposition of Mr. Arnold who remained on the committee.

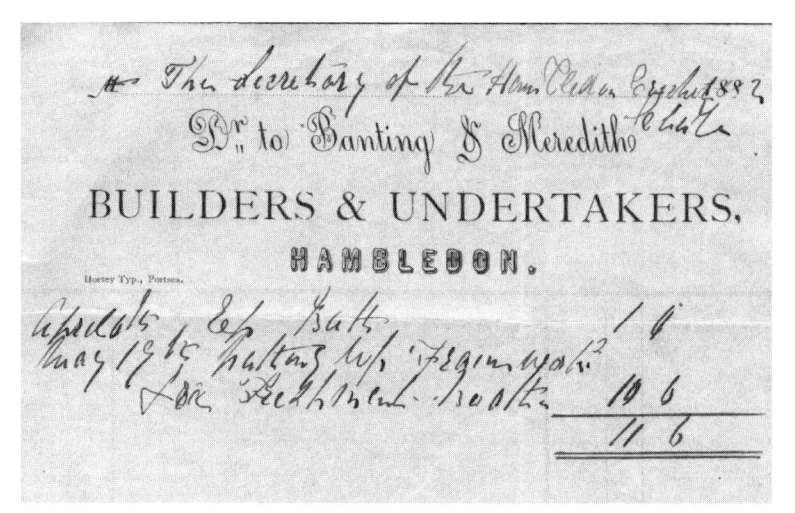

Meredith was an early supporter of the Club, while the Bantings played right through to the 1970s. The firm built the first pavilion in 1881.

At the only two committee meetings held in 1880, the main issue was whether the club should rent a meadow with a view to subletting it and making some money on the deal. They approached J.F. Higgens but eventually it was a Vice President, Mr. Hatfield who hired a field from Mr. Courtney at £7.10.0 (£7.50) a year. That winter an entertainment was held on behalf of the club and in the spring they fixed practice nights on Tuesdays, Thursdays and Saturdays at 5pm. As the next scorebook will show, the club's matches were all day ones played on almost any day of the week other than Saturdays and Sundays and it was to be almost 75 years before there was any cricket on the Sabbath.

Early in 1881 the committee resolved to build a pavilion adjoining the cricket ground. Messrs Banting and Meredith were the builders and they had completed their work by May when the building was transferred to Captain Butler to be held for the club as a yearly tenant as the minute says, "Under the College of Winchester" and it was insured with contents for £50. This long serving building did indeed adjoin the ground for it lay outside the field granted for recreational purposes. When the club eventually replaced it in 1969, they had to put up the new one on a different site within their own boundary.

These rapid developments are followed by a jolt; the next recorded meeting was not until September and that, general, meeting was adjourned to January 1882. The outcome is lost. Then there is a gap of 11 pages before you come upon lists of members and subscriptions for the years 1878 to 1881. They began with 46 members among them W.K. Wright, H. and C. Banting, H. Smith, J. and F. Crook, Fastrudge, Lay, W. and F. Cole, W. Slowe, H. and W. May, E. Beagley, H. Hooker, W. Taylor and W. Tanner. The sub was 5 shillings (25p): nearly as many paid the following year, but there is a dropping off in 1880 and 1881. There is also a list of subscribers who must have been non-playing members. Some have the suffix "Esq.". Mr. Gaman is just that, so is Mr. Gunn and there are six female subscribers, a number of clerics and Henty and Co. the brewers.

The balance sheet for 1878 showed that there had indeed been a reformation of the club as the first three items on the debit side are

	£	s	d
Account book and stationery	5	2	
Cricketing gear and carriage of same	6	17	6
Printing and carriage of rules		8	0

while there are items reminiscent of the days on Windmill Down such as payment for umpire and scorer 5 shillings and 5/6d; mowing and sweeping ground 1/9d and (the first of many such references) *Returning roller 1/0d*

The income from 45 playing members was £11.5.0 and other items totalled £20. Deducting expenditure of £9.14.4, the clubs balance in hand was £10.5.8.

This reduced to 54 pence in the following year but had improved to a little under £9 by the end of 1881 as shown in an elegantly printed annual report and set of accounts. The club's funds were boosted by the profits of an entertainment early the following year. In February 1882 Mr. Best received a vote of thanks for his services on his retirement from the post of secretary, Captain Butler was in the chair, E. Goldsmith was treasurer and F. Crook secretary.

In March the club authorised the Rev W. Maynard of Horndean Cricket Club to engage Jackman as a professional bowler for the summer, the Hambledon committee guaranteeing £18 as their half share of the expense. More than this, three weeks later they also took on the Hampshire professional F.G. Willoughby as groundsman for the two clubs for 18 weeks at £2 a week. Frederick George Willoughby born in Edinburgh on 25 April 1862 was a left arm medium paced bowler who played eight first class matches for Hampshire in 1885 taking 25 wickets average 22. He died in Winchester in 1952.

HAMBLEDON CRICKET CLUB,

1882.

President:
Captain THOMAS BUTLER.

Vice-President:
W. H. HATFIELD, Esq.

Committee:

Major HALE. J. TWYNAM, Esq.
Mr. A. ARNOLD. Mr. H. MEREDITH.
Mr. J. KNIGHT. Mr. J. B. STEVENSON.

Treasurer:
E. GOLDSMITH, Esq.

Honorary Secretary:
Mr. F. CROOK.

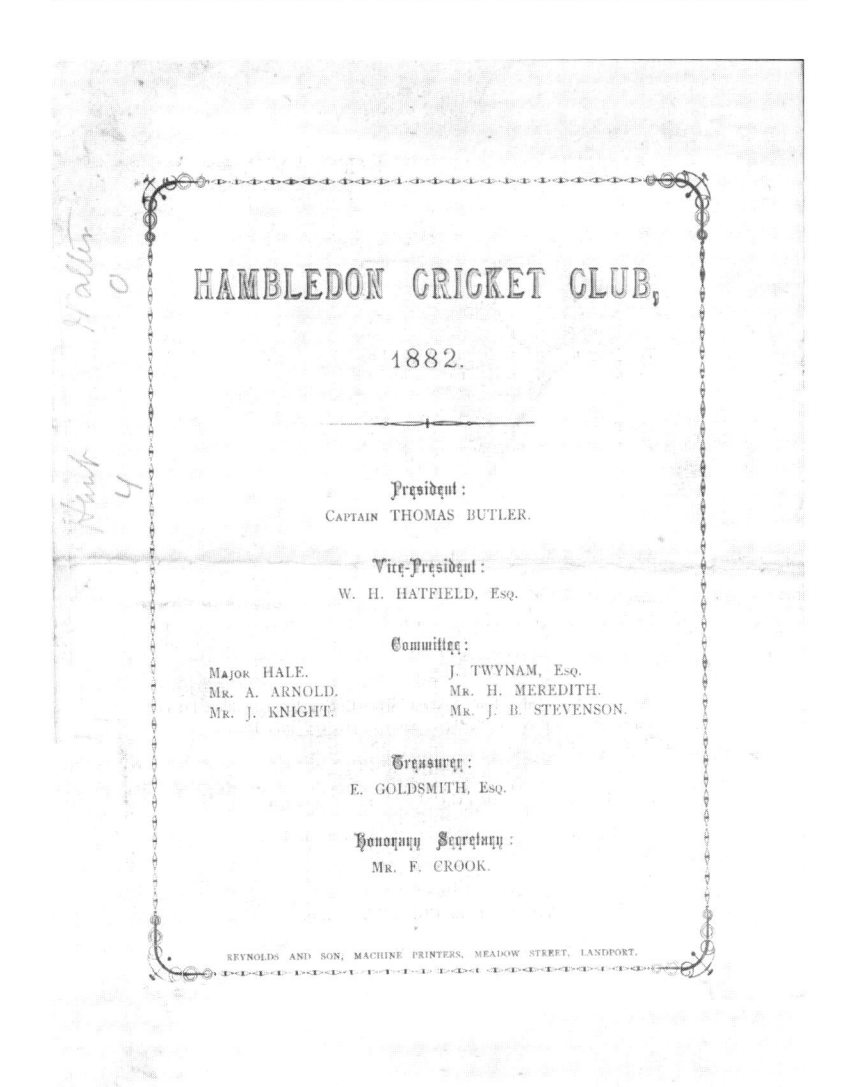

REYNOLDS AND SON, MACHINE PRINTERS, MEADOW STREET, LANDPORT.

The grandly printed annual report and accounts for 1882

All this activity may have been over ambitious as trouble soon arose and at a meeting of the committee on 23 November 1882 at which Captain Butler presided supported by Major Hale, A. Arnold, E. Goldsmith, J.B. Stevenson and the secretary Mr. Crook this resolution was carried:

> *That before any matches are made, or any professional engaged, a meeting of the committee shall be held and until the secretary has reported to the committee the amount of subscriptions for the year either already paid or promised NO MATCHES shall be made, or any engagement entered into.*

Clearly some member or members of the club had been exceeding their authority and the clubs finances had suffered. Perhaps those at the meeting were the ones who had to make good the loss. There are no surviving accounts or balance sheets for 1883 and the remaining 14 pages of the minute book are blank. Mr. Best must have been sorely missed.

Following that crisis we come to a scorebook covering the season of 1884, but as on examination it turns out to be the Horndean CC book, the scores are not as informative as a Hambledon supporter or historian would wish. The last match of the season was against Hambledon and the books must have been exchanged by mistake. Horndean at least provide evidence that Hambledon were playing that year whatever may have happened in 1882 or 1883, but the presence of the book shows how dependent on chance we are for our knowledge of activity in the fairly distant past.

The two sides had also met at Horndean in May when J. Goldsmith, A. Arnold and F. Hartridge were in the Hambledon team. Five balls were bowled to the over although in first class cricket the number did not increase from four until 1889 (there was an increase to six balls an over eleven years later). Earlier in that season of 1884 Horndean played Southsea Rovers whose team included Dr. Doyle - A. Conan Doyle.

Chapter 6
Turn Of The Century

The story now moves forward into the 1890s with the club scorebook for 1891 soon followed by a gargantuan minute book running on from April 1894 to 1907. In 1891 Hambledon played 14 matches winning six and losing eight. There were also two games against Havant Juniors, the first won by Hambledon on the first innings, and the second a tie with 57 runs a side. These like the ones played by the adults were all day games continuing on to a second innings. A feature of the two colts fixtures was the bowling of F. Holmes (not an invention of Conan Doyle) whose analyses of 5 for 16 and 5 for 34 in the first were followed by 7 for 23 and 4 for 12 in the return match. He did not develop into a regular member of the team but other names in the junior side did become familiar: E. Lunn, A. May, Parvin and Hartridge.

In a match between Hambledon Sunflowers and Hambledon, occurs for the first time the name of W. Langridge, who worked as a domestic groom and was an outstanding all round cricketer for many years, but did not always offer his services to his home club. In this match, as a precursor of many future successes he seized six wickets for 11 runs and four more for six runs in the second innings. The club's season began with three successive victories over Bishops Waltham, Meon Valley and Havant, games in which no innings total reached three figures, indeed in the Havant match the scoring was low indeed as Hambledon's scores of 42 and 39 were sufficient to beat the opposition whose totals were 46 and 31. It is a pity there are no bowling figures to relish. When Hambledon met Havant Redstar their score of 90 was not good enough in the face of their opponents 112.

A typical seniors side of that season included W. Henstridge, H. Hooker, W.G. Rapsom, W. Langridge, J. Twynam, C. Carter, A. Arnold, S. Dancaster, E. Palmer, C. Woodger and E. March.
After defeating Purbrook on 17 June (Langridge 3 for 12 and four for 24), they lost six matches on the trot and that lean spell was followed by only two further victories.

Langridge took eight for 38 against Purbrook who nevertheless won this return match by an innings scoring 104 to Hambledon's totals of 20 and 56. Not a single individual score of over 50 was made for Hambledon, although it must be said that only one was scored against them but H. Garman finished the season with scores of 48 against Fareham 2nd XI and 39 against Horndean.

There is then a gap again before the minute book continues the tale in 1894. The club held a concert that April and the minutes refer to the employment of Mr. Chase to convey teams to out matches, white coats for the umpires and payment for Gunn and Moore's accounts for gear. The officers for the following season were named as:

President Captain Butler
Vice Presidents Captain Adderley, Dr. Jeram and T. Lee Esq.
Captain E.F.W. Lunn. Vice Captain Mr. E. Palmer
The committee were C. Carter, Mr. Bendall, H. Banting Snr., W. Budd, Jno Knight and W. Henstridge. E.P. Durrant was Hon Treasurer and the Hon. Secretary was Edgar Lunn.

On March 15 1895 begins a series of minutes which continues unbroken up to 1926. Some quotations give their flavour.
15 March 1895 Mr.C. Carter in the chair and Messrs W. Henstridge, Ed Palmer, E.J.W. Lunn and J. Knight present who were appointed to meet and arrange what repairs should be done to the ground. It was proposed by Mr. Carter and seconded by Mr. Henstridge that the secretary instruct H. Turner to repair net. The sec to purchase 1/2 doz balls at 4/9d (24.5 pence), new minute book, also new receipt book for treasurer and look through club gear and have necessary repairs done. As soon as list of matches completed, sec to get 100 fixture cards printed and sent out to honary (sic) members.
Good old secretary!

H. Turner who had only one leg and was known as Stumps was scorer for the club for 48 years up to 1934 and was grandfather of Robert (Topsy) Turner, who has been a fine player for Hambledon for over 40 years, as we shall see. Although in later years when costume matches were played, Stumps kept score by cutting notches into a stick he normally recorded the scores in a clear hand in the scorebook.

17 May 1895 at The George Inn. Present Jno Knight in the chair and Messrs C. Bendall, W. Budd, Ed. Durrant, E.J.W. Lunn, C. Carter, E. Lunn. Proposed by Mr. Carter, seconded by Mr. Bendall that the junior members paying less than three shillings (15 pence) should practice by themselves on Monday and Wednesday nights and that the captain be asked that some senior member be always present for instruction purposes. Proposed Mr. Carter, seconded Mr. Lunn that W. Chase be engaged for conveyance to out matches at 16 shillings (80 pence) per journey. The sec was instructed to arrange matches

Charles Briggs and his family: supporters of the club before the First World War

with the Sergeants of the R. Artillery in place of the two East Meon matches which had been scratched. Periodically the full committee met to select teams for several fixtures. A constant source of discussion was the state of the pavilion as even in those days vandalism was a problem: in June 1895 there was a break in, while at successive meetings in September, Mr. Banting the builder was asked to submit an estimate for repairs and repainting and in the spring of 1896 the committee put up a large printed notice on the pavilion that "any person or persons damaging this pavilion or the fences will be prosecuted by order of the committee."

It soon became the custom to hold a general meeting after the end of the season, initially in January of the following year but subsequently earlier in the autumn, and another one in March. John Knight was always in the chair until in 1897 Edward Whalley-Tooker began to share the duties. The first reference to his name occurs on 31 January 1896 when he was elected captain. He had previously served in a similar capacity for Denmead Cricket Club. Born in 1863 he was descended from two ancient families associated with the club in the XVIII Century, the Whalleys and the Tookers. He was not in the eleven at Eton but had played once for Hampshire in 1882 against Sussex at the Antelope Ground, Southampton: the invitation read, "The nearest station is Northam. We shall begin about 12". His family were landowners in a big way in the Hambledon area. In June 1896 the committee passed a resolution congratulating him on his marriage to Miss Dorothy Charnock of Whitedale. He proved indispensable to the Hambledon Cricket Club for more than 40 years. He and his elder brother, Hyde, had ancestral links with Sir Nicholas Hyde who was chief justice of the Kings Bench in the XVI Century and his nephew Edward Hyde, Earl of Clarendon, Lord Chancellor in the reign of Charles II. There was little which went on in and around Hambledon in which Edward was not involved.

He may not have received the best of initial impressions when the club's auditors were tersely ordered to "attend their duty at once". Another appearance was that of H. Hooker as a committee member. His family were also for a long time connected with the club.

In 1897 fixtures were arranged with Clanfield, East Meon, Horndean, R.A. Sergeants, Meon Valley, Soberton, R.A. Hilsea, Idsworth, Bordean and Waterloo.

A new Vice President was the recently inducted vicar, The Rev. H.C. Floud who was destined to play a large part in the affairs of the club. The season began with a hat trick by H. Budd against Clanfield, for which he was presented not with a cap but with a cup. A week or so later on 10 May the committee selected these players to play in the return match against Clanfield:

G. Batts, H. Budd, A. May, F. Hurst, E.W. Tooker, F. Collis, E. Hartridge, Ireland, F. Parvin, W. Langridge and J. Joyce.

Later in the month a proposal that H. Budd, W. Langridge and F. Parvin should be paid lunch expenses when playing in full day matches was referred to a general meeting where it was carried by six votes to five. Fees or expenses were also discussed in relation to A. Bendall who was asked to play for the club that season "on the same terms as last year." Mr. Penny took over the transport of the team instead of Mr. Chase (who however recovered the contract in the following year) at 16/- shillings (80 pence) a journey. The purchase of a bag for the gear cost 12 shillings (60 pence). For the first time a grounds committee was formed consisting of Messrs Banting, Hooker, H. Budd and H. Turner. Soon a new flag was called for, four feet long and three feet wide, the design being blue ground with a white border three inches deep.

There seems nothing controversial in a proposal to mow the grass on the cricket field, but three weeks after the committee approved it, Mr. Whalley-Tooker had to propose that a letter of apology be sent to the club's landlord Mr. Taylor and the copy in the minute book reads "We the undersigned being members of the HCC beg to apologise for our mistake in cutting grass on cricket ground without your consent and will do our best to meet you in any way you think fair.
Signed: E. Whalley-Tooker (chair), John Knight, Henry Banting, E.F.W. Lunn, Hon Sec HCC"
No doubt the farmer was anxious to preserve his grazing rights, an attitude which Mr. Whalley-Tooker would fully understand.

In February 1898, the firm, clear writing of J.A. Best appears in the minute book. An accountant by training, it is said that for a time he ran a private school at the top of the High Street near the church. He subsequently became collector of taxes for the parish and assistant clerk to the parish council. His first act was to record a dispute about the chairmanship of the meeting. A proposal that Mr. Batts take the chair resulted in a tie at three votes each. John Knight who chaired the start of the meeting had seconded the proposition. An amendment that he be appointed chairman resulted in another tie and was carried "by the casting vote". It is not clear who, by that time, was occupying the chair and the proceedings were hardly a vote of confidence but Mr. Knight continued to chair committee meetings after that.

Edward Whalley-Tooker (seated) and J.A. Best, Captain and Hon Secretary at the turn of the 19th century

There were further signs of discontent in June when the club was still looking to complete that seasons fixture list, while early in July there was a dispute in committee about team selection: should that committee select the teams to play Idsworth and Waterloo? The chairman, Mr. Knight, gave his second and casting vote in favour of the motion. If club members remained dissatisfied about the way the teams were selected, they kept quiet about it from then on. More positively, towards the end of the season, H. Budd took his second hat trick and the club presented him with a cap and badge.

There were no meetings between the one on 22 October 1898, which was adjourned for a week and not resumed, and a general meeting on 9 February 1899. On that occasion the members decided not to play Clanfield again, in spite of an amendment by Mr. Whalley-Tooker. His wise counsel prevailed however and the motion was rescinded a fortnight later. There was further controversy in store as in April the committee resolved to transfer the clubhouse from the George to the New Inn. An amendment in favour of The Bat and Ball was rejected by three votes to seven. Then again on 29 May they voted to ask H. Hooker to resign his position as a member of the committee "and hand over all the property of the club to the ground committee". Something unpleasant must have occurred at the next match as a week later they confirmed that the motion be enforced and that entry to the scoring tent be restricted and after a further week, determined to start legal proceedings against Mr. Hooker, presumably because he had failed to return the club's property. There is no indication as to how the dispute was settled.

The only achievement on the field in 1899 which was noted in the minutes was W. Langridge's hat trick against the 20 Company Royal Artillery. At the general meeting on 5 March 1900 he was elected Vice Captain. For that season the series of scorebooks resumes and we can try and assess the playing strength of the club. In 1900 they played 15 matches, winning seven and losing eight; because the matches were all day ones and scoring continued to be low, many years were to pass before draws became a feature. They began with a splendid win over Waterlooville, W. Hartridge's 44 proving crucial to a victory by 45 runs, but they sustained three loses in the next four matches, the most inglorious being that against Alliance on 4 June when the oppositions total of 92 was far too large for Hambledon who replied with 23 and 42. Those two totals completed a run by the club of five consecutive innings of less than 100 runs, which, following one match when they reached the coveted three figures was followed by a further seven failures. The match with Droxford on 20 June stands out like a beacon as Hambledon scored 200 for five declared, E. Whalley-Tooker 67, Wiggington 45, W. Twynam 27, F. Collis 25 and F. Golding 24 not out. Droxford could only reply with 62, Golding completing a good all round performance by taking eight wickets for 39. Further low scoring then led to four additional consecutive defeats, before the season ended more cheerfully with three wins on the trot. Golding turned in several fine, if not match winning, performances including seven for 10 and six for five against G.M.J. (Fareham) and seven for 53 and six for 33 against Waterlooville, followed by six for 29 v. Droxford, all in consecutive innings. W. Langridge took seven wickets for 42 for the captains XI against the club. Alf Turner was another young cricketer to show promise.

Results were very similar in 1901 with seven wins as against six defeats. Runs remained very hard to get and Hambledon reached the three-figure mark only four times during the season. A. Hughes, 55, was the only batsman to reach the heights of a half century: luckily, as may be judged from the quality of Hambledon's attack, opponents found runs hard to come by as well, except for Stanstead who won both home and away after scoring 217 for four and 245 - against Hambledon's totals of 93 and 56.

The main feature of 1901 was the formation of the Bishops Waltham district and parish cricket league, which Hambledon joined in April. It is not possible to distinguish the league games from the other fixtures but it is interesting to note that even with this participation, Hambledon played fewer matches that year. The minutes do not refer to any great success in the league, indeed the only reference to it came at a general meeting in October when the club resolved to continue its connection with the league, "provided Bishops Waltham find a proper ground on which return matches are to be played…"

A little acrimony carried over into the new year for at the general meeting on 19 February 1902 there was an dispute about who should be Vice Chairman, when W. Durrant proposed and Mr. Whalley-Tooker seconded Mr. Hughes for the post which was one of increasing importance as Mr. Whalley-Tooker who had mostly replaced John Knight was often unavailable for committee meetings: however Mr. Hartridge was elected by a majority of nine to six. A subsequent resolution that Mr. Hughes should not act as the carrier to away matches was defeated. What he had done to cause offence was not recorded. A year later it is noted that he had "left the village".

There were no committee meetings recorded between 25 July and 24 November 1902. This may be because the season ended early (it was one of the wettest on record with 1903 a close comparator) and there was no need to select teams rather than for any sinister reason: there are however no scores available between 1901 and 1904 and no minutes for 1905. Up to that season we get such detail as we can from the minute book.

1902 ended with a dinner on 11 December while in the following February the committee resolved to present W. Langridge with a bat. Hambledon must have finished top of the league as in November 1903 Mr. Hartridge was asked to take custody of the league cup until

The membership, and ex-membership list, 1906

arrangements had been made for the trophy to be kept securely at The New Inn. This confirms that the club had changed its headquarters from the George and only after the club had opened its new pavilion in 1969 was another change made. Late in the summer of 1903 there were problems with opposing sides, the committee agreeing not to play the return match with Waterlooville and then passing a resolution that Portsmouth Rugby Club pay all expenses for .... failing to meet their engagement. In 1904 there was an unsuccessful attempt to start a junior team with an age limit of seventeen. After a month the idea was deferred and the club returned the subscriptions which had been paid.

There are no minutes between 1 July 1904 and 15 March 1905 when only nine members attended a general meeting at which however there is no indication of any concern about fixtures or playing strength or finance. There are no minutes of committee meetings at all for the rest of that year which is strange as a full seasons cricket was played in 1905 and it proved to be one of the most successful on record, showing 15 matches played, 11 won, three lost and one tie. That summer marked a real transformation in the fortunes of the club as they continually showed better form than almost all their opponents with the exception of Leigh Park who were successful in both their matches. Hambledon undoubtedly benefited from the presence of Dr. Court the medical officer and surgeon who bowled successfully in almost every game he played, while F. Singleton and H. Chase also return good analyses. The season began with a handsome victory over Bishops Waltham, who scored only 58 (Singleton six wickets for 29, Court four for 29) against Hambledon's 119. Court and P. Sabin returned even better figures in the dismissal of Soberton for 36, Dr. Court contributing 50 to Hambledon's total of 120 which gave them an easy victory. The two victories over Meon Valley, who must have been rather weak, produced staggering figures: Hambledon's 90 (Court 32) sufficed for victory by an innings, as the opposition totalled 11 with

Court	4.1 overs,	no maidens,	9 runs,	5 wickets
Singleton	4,	3,	1,	4;
and 64				
Court	6,	2,	18,	4
Singleton	5.5,	4,	4,	2

In the return match, Meon Valley did not fare quite as well, as they were dismissed for 10 (Court five for six) after which Hambledon enjoyed the remainder of the day with their score at 212, Sabin 62, Langridge 44, J. Allen 34 and Dr. Court 25. In mid summer they tied with Bishops Waltham at 43 a side, Court 9 overs, 2 maidens, 12 runs, 8 wickets.

After that they won seven games out of nine, this pleasant period being interrupted only by the two defeats by Leigh Park. The first was quite narrow the scores being 103 to 89, but the return fixture resulted in a hiding by 188 to 117 in spite of an innings of 37 by H. Chase who was in good all round form at this time.

Only one 2nd XI match is recorded which Barn Green won by 76 to Hambledon's 33. C. Hooker took six wickets.

It is a disappointment that there is only one recorded match for 1906 in which the club continued their run of success with a win over Denmead, the Rev H.A. Floud being undefeated for 36. Then the run of scores is broken and the minutes for 1906 are scanty as well.

The reasons for the lack of detail around this time are unclear but what does emerge is that 1907 was another successful season, beginning with the drubbing of Droxford. Fortunately for morale a defeat by Clanfield was followed by successes in seven of the eight games played in June, July and August with one draw intervening.

Scores remained very low but at this time opponents totals were lower still: Hambledon 49, Meon Valley 26; Hambledon 52, Denmead 16 and Hambledon 36, Soberton 30 being cases in point. The Rev Floud contributed a number of good scores in the second half of the season including 58 not out against Bishops Waltham, 43 versus Swanmore and 87 in the match with Soberton when Hambledon's total rose to the height of 171 for eight enabling them to win by 103. W. Langridge again contributed useful all round performances and G. Hall returned figures of six for 23 in a narrow win over Meon Valley and eight for 31 to defeat Droxford. E. Hartridge and F. Sealey made helpful scores.

Cricket Club 1906 Sheet

Expenditure

		£	s	d	£	s	d
Deficit Balance from 1905 now paid	Late Treasurer	3	6	10½			
	Gunn & Moore	5	15	2			
	H. W. Knight		6	0	9	8	0½
Presentation Cricket Boots — 1905						11	0
Subscription to League						5	0
E. J. Taylor — repairs						7	0
W. Langridge — labour on ground					3	11	6
H. Turner — scoring					2	10	0
F. Fuller — new Gear					7	13	8
Laundry — washing Umpires' Coats						1	0
W. E. Hunt — Printing						14	0
Win: Colb: — Rent of Pavilion Site						2	6
F. Kemp — Hire & Umpires' Teas					4	5	0
B. Goffin — whitening & oil							7½
Assist: Sec: — postage						1	0
H. W. Knight — net cord, repairs, &c.						12	4
Balance in hand					1	9	10
					31	12	6

Francis Hashidgs
Fred Samways

Finance 1906

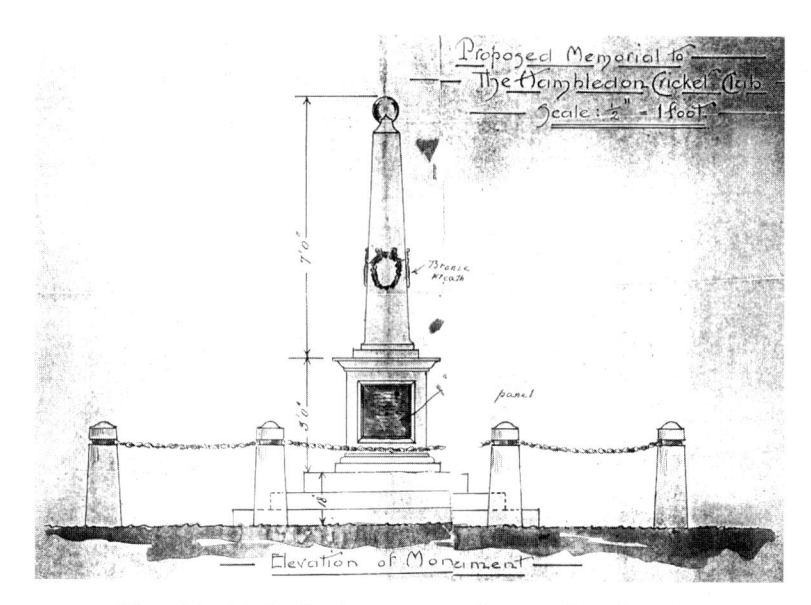

The original design for the monument: Bertram Cancellor 1908

Chapter 7
The Route To The Monument

Altogether the general meeting held on 15 October 1907 had plenty of grounds for enthusiasm. They were inspired on the proposition of Edward Whalley-Tooker, seconded by Mr. Best to vote for the erection of a memorial "on the site of the original ground". The germ of this idea had first come forward in July 1906 when a general meeting of the club agreed to accept a challenge to play a side of Veterans of England, the Hambledon club to be 18 players, but nothing came of this. The meeting in October 1907 went on to set up a sub-committee consisting of Captain Butler, Whalley-Tooker, The Rev Floud, J.A. Best and J. Knight. They met three times in October and November and as a result Mr. Floud wrote to the owner of Broadhalfpenny Down for permission to erect the memorial opposite the porch of The Bat and Ball. Bertram Cancellor, the Winchester architect, furnished a design in the form of a classical column, which would have been a real adornment to Broadhalfpenny Down. When the elegance of the pillar did not meet with the approval of the committee who asked him to design something "of a simpler character" he hastily prepared a rough sketch, which is a reflection of the base of King Alfred's statue in Winchester, which was the concept of the sculptor Hamo Thornycroft. The club accepted this less expensive design, and land agents in Hull representing the Pease family, the owners of the Down, soon approved the proposal. Captain Butler drafted a letter inviting subscriptions from all the first class counties, Oxford and Cambridge Universities, the principal clubs of Scotland and Ireland, the Philadelphia Club, USA, and many others, but money did not flow in as rapidly as the committee hoped and in April 1908 they had to agree to provide four guarantors at £10 each before work on the monument could begin and they had to make renewed appeals for donations through the press. By the end of May their efforts were sufficiently successful for the club to accept the architects design and give the go ahead. The simple inscription [see page 10 above] was, as Ashley Mote has suggested, drawn up during a junior Hambledon match.

It always seems to have been the intention that the inauguration of the monument should be carried out as part of a cricket festival on Broadhalfpenny Down. In a lengthy report after the matches played in September 1908, the Hampshire Chronicle reported that the wicket had been laid in the previous November by members of the Hambledon club using turf from the neighbouring down under the supervision of the groundsman at the County Ground, Southampton, Jesse Hopkins. He made several visits to the Down during the summer of 1908. The time and effort needed to prepare Broadhalfpenny Down for four days of cricket, the three day first class match followed by a one day game, when there had been no cricket at all there since 1792, must have been immense and have required all Hopkins' skill to produce the finished product but the scores show that the results of his efforts were more than adequate.

It comes as a surprise that the earliest reference to team selection in the Hambledon minutes comes as late as 28 July 1908, when at a general meeting 23 members of the club agreed that (1) only members of the club should form the committee for the cricket festival and that (2) the two representatives of Hambledon in the team of that name should be members of the club or that they should be Hambledon born. These were clearly significant responses to an impetus coming from outside the club. The leading light was undoubtedly C.B. Fry who was actively involved in the preparations for the Hambledon versus All-England match, the majority of which must have already been in place before the club's deliberations at the end of July. Edward Whalley-Tooker and W. Langridge were in the event selected as the two club representatives in the team, which played under the heading of "Hambledon", and they appear with the Hampshire professionals and other players in the team photographs; Whalley-Tooker was captain. The match was fixed for 10,11 and 12 September 1908 and was followed by a one-day game on the 14th.

Fry was by this time, with his Sussex colleague, Kumar Shri Ranjitsinjhi, the best known cricketer in England following a dozen seasons of success with his adopted county (he was born in Surrey and had his first county trial with them), and with England although his triumphs at the highest level were less consistently achieved. Fry held almost every batting record at a time when interest in statistics was reaching the peak which it has maintained ever since. In 1900 he amassed a hundred and a double hundred in one match against Surrey at Hove, a feat not repeated in first class cricket for nearly twenty years, and in the following season hit six hundreds in successive innings, a performance which he came near to repeating in 1911 with a further four in succession. By the end of his career, in India in 1921/22, he had reached three figures on 94 occasions. In 1901 his aggregate of

Poster for the All-England match, 1908

runs for the season, 3,147, had been exceeded only by Ranji in 1899, although Bobby Abel of Surrey also beat Ranji's total in 1901. Fry's 13 centuries in that season remained a record until 1925 when Jack Hobbs beat it. An equally amazing achievement was his average of 81 in 1903 a notoriously wet season when run getting was very difficult. His total that year was 2,683 runs. In 1912 he captained England in the Triangular Tournament against Australia and South Africa with unblemished success.

He was already living in Hampshire, and in 1909 while he was still the elected captain of Sussex, he transferred his allegiance in county cricket to Hampshire where his wife had already assumed responsibility for running the Training Ship Mercury at Hamble.

The fact remains that there is no reference to Fry at all in the Hambledon minutes. There is a reference to HRH Prince Edward of Wales, subsequently King Edward VIII, then aged 14, who was invited to unveil the memorial, or failing him (and he failed) W.G. Grace or Captain Butler. When on the day, W.G. could not make the journey following an injury while playing cricket, it was E.M. Sprot, the Hampshire County captain who, after being introduced by Captain Butler, performed the unveiling ceremony.

The occasion and the three-day match were described at length in the Hampshire Chronicle, whose correspondent estimated the attendance on the first day before lunch at 3,000 people, increasing to 5,000 in the afternoon. Nominal charges were made for seats in the enclosure: motorists readily paid five shillings (25p) for driving onto the ground, single horsed vehicles were charged two shillings (10p) and double that for two horses. The cost of cycle storage was three pence (one and a half pence) and there were 680 of them in the racks. Luncheon for the public was provided in two marquees erected by Salters of Winchester with a bar while there was separate provision for the teams and officials, the press and the band, which was provided by the Training Ship Mercury. All were at risk from devastatingly high winds sweeping across the exposed heights - indeed two tents were blown down before the start of play.

The committee entertained the teams to lunch in their separate marquee where Captain Butler presided. On the top table were displayed two punch bowls and twelve plates originally used by the old Hambledon Club, which had been loaned by Hyde Whalley-Tooker, the captain's brother. After speeches by Captain Butler, who went out of his way to thank C.B. Fry to whose untiring efforts and energy the existence of the match was due; by E.M. Sprot and Gilbert Jessop of Gloucestershire, who provoked laughter by his translation of an alleged early Celtic reference to the game as "better not to break ones neck, but better to crick it" they moved across the Down to the memorial which Sprot unveiled amid further speech making.

Most of the earnest verbiage of Captain Butler and the Archdeacon of Winchester the Venerable W.A. Fearon was blown away by the continuing high wind over Broadhalfpenny Down as almost was the tarpaulin as it was pulled off the monument.

The match itself was given first-class status although the teams

Gilbert Jessop (seated), Edward Whalley-Tooker and E.M. Sprot after the unveiling of the monument.

played twelve a side, and the play proved worthy of the occasion, All-England fighting back when they batted a second time, 153 runs behind Hambledon on the first innings. Several well known players, including Jessop, scored freely second time around, but the top scorer was George Leach, the Sussex fast bowler, who hit 80 in quick time before Langridge, who was given a good spell with the ball, dismissed him. Fry showed the seriousness with which he treated the match by batting in determined fashion for his unbeaten 84 which ensured victory for Hambledon.

Probably the happiest participant was the young Jack Newman of Hampshire with 13 wickets in the match which contributed to his career total of 2056 wickets between 1906 and 1930, while the Rev W.V. Jephson, who recorded his sole first-class hundred in the match must also have been very proud, although it must be added that he did a lot of useful batting for Hampshire over the dozen years before the First World War.

The village was bedecked with flags and bunting hung across the village streets and an air of festivity prevailed. For several days after the match large crowds turned up to view the memorial stone. Yet when it came to finalising the accounts a fortnight later, this grand event resulted in virtually no profit, because of the expense of the preparation of the wicket, the hiring of accommodation on the ground, and printing and publicity.

The final account showed:

Receipts £112.4.0
Expenditure £111.5.1
Profit .... £0.18.11 (95 pence)!

There was talk of maintaining the centre of the ground in the hope of encouraging the Australian tourists of 1909 to come and play, but this did not happen.

Hambledon continued their play at Brook Lane.

The references to the great match in the minutes are very brief: soon afterwards the club agreed to fence the memorial and to have it photographed while in October they paid Mr. Cancellor's fee of 5 guineas (£5.25). After the match the club held a supper and smoking concert, to celebrate their victory and to make a presentation to J.A. Best who in reply gave details of his connection with the club as player and secretary going back over 30 years. Mr. Whalley-Tooker was presented with the bat he used in the match while the six balls were given to Captain Butler, G.L. Jessop, E.M. Sprot, Mr. Best, F.H. Bacon (Secretary of Hampshire CCC) and Jesse Hopkins. In turn Mr. Whalley-Tooker presented to the club a set of stumps and bails used in the game, which were to be enclosed in a glass case, presumably at the New Inn. Hambledon had every reason to celebrate: the village and the club had been well and truly restored to the cricketing map.

CHAPTER 7

Before the All-England match, 1908 at North End House, Droxford. First Row left to right: Jack Newman, Phil Mead, unknown lady, unknown man, Albert Trott (seated), behind him Ewart Astill. Behind to right: A.E. Knight, and far right, J.Stone.

The Hambledon Team v. All-England. Back row: Phil Mead, Jack Newman and Charles Llewellyn. Centre: J. Stone (in boater), W. Langridge, C.B. Fry, Major E.G. Wynyard, Ron W.V. Jephson. Front. E.M.C. Ede, Capt. T.D. Butler, E. Whalley-Tooker, E.M.Sprot, G.N. Bignell (who played as G.N. Deer).

– 61 –

Other Matches.

HAMBLEDON v. AN ENGLAND TEAM.

Played at HAMBLEDON, *Thursday, Friday, Saturday, September* 10, 11, 12.— For the first time for more than a hundred years Broad Half-penny Down was the scene of a game between elevens styled Hambledon and An England Team. The match proved a great attraction and we have C. B. Fry's enthusiastic testimony to the keenness with which it was played. On the opening day a granite column commemorating the glories of the Hambledon Club was unveiled, the necessary funds having been raised by public subscription. In the absence of W. G. Grace the unveiling ceremony was performed by E. M. Sprot, the Hampshire captain. After being 153 behind on the first innings the England Team pulled the game round but in the end Hambledon won by five wickets, Fry playing in his finest form for 84 not out.

AN ENGLAND TEAM.

A. E. Knight b Llewellyn	9	— b Deer b Newman	13
Mr. A. W. Roberts b Newman	11	— Newman	69
E. H. Killick b Newman	7	— run out	2
J. T. Hearne b Newman	4	— b Newman	2
Mr. F. G. J. Ford c and b Newman	33	— c Newman b Llewellyn	7
Mr. G. Wilder b Newman	0	— b Newman	43
Mr. G. L. Jessop b Newman	19	— st Stone b Llewellyn	48
A. E. Trott c Mead b Newman	4	— c Mead b Llewellyn	5
G. Leach lbw. b Llewellyn	2	— c Wynyard b Langridge	80
G. Dennett not out	28	— b Llewellyn	4
H. R. Butt b Newman	3	— c Fry b Newman	9
W. E. Astill run out	1	— not out	8
L-b 1, n-b 2	3	B 7, l-b 8, w 2, n-b 2	19
	124		**309**

HAMBLEDON.

Mr. C. B. Fry b Hearne	17	— not out	84
Capt. E. G. Wynyard c Hearne b Dennett	59	— not out	9
Mr. E. M. Sprot c Wilder b Astill	9	— c Trott b Jessop	17
J. B. Llewellyn c Trott b Astill	0	— b Hearne	2
Rev. W. V. Jephson not out	114	— st Butt b Dennett	14
Mr. G. N. Deer b Roberts	10		
P. Mead b Dennett	0	— c Trott b Hearne	6
A. Stone c Trott b Killick	6	— b Astill	2
Mr. E. Whalley-Tooker b Killick	6		
Mr. W. Langridge b Dennett	2		
Mr. E. M. C. Ede b Killick	4		
J. Newman c and b Killick	23	— c and b Astill	5
B 25, l-b 1, n-b 1	27	B 11, l-b 7, n-b 1	19
	277		**158**

HAMBLEDON BOWLING.

	Overs	Mdns.	Runs	Wkts.	Overs	Mdns.	Runs	Wkts.
Newman	15.5	1	54	8	17.3	2	66	5
Llewellyn	12	1	60	2	26	3	133	4
Deer	3	0	7	0	3	0	11	0
Mead					10	1	38	0
Langridge					14	2	42	1

AN ENGLAND TEAM'S BOWLING.

	Overs	Mdns.	Runs	Wkts.	Overs	Mdns.	Runs	Wkts.
Hearne	9	0	31	1	11	1	32	2
Astill	5	0	23	2	9	0	33	2
Leach	3	0	15	0				
Trott	10	0	45	0	2	0	6	0
Killick	10.3	2	44	4	4.3	2	13	0
Jessop	4	0	9	0	13	5	30	1
Dennett	17	0	74	3	9	0	25	1
Roberts	2	0	9	1				

Umpires: Tuck and W. Pate.

Wisden's report on the match.

CHAPTER 8

Before A Fall

The club's own domestic season of 1908 opened on an unhappy note with an offer of resignation from the Hon. Secretary, the Rev Floud. In addition to his pastoral duties he had been heavily involved in the initial preparations for the All-England match, to the exclusion perhaps of his other work for the club as only in March did the committee discuss what fixtures there were for the coming season. Subsequently he was persuaded to continue in office and in the fixture list, which was in spite of the late start, increased to 21 matches apart from the All-England match, the club had 12 victories to set against eight defeats. There was only one drawn game. The results would have been even better, but for a horrendous start in which the batting proved ineffective in three of the first four games. When Meon Valley were put out for 15 at the end of May, R.C. Atkins figures were 6 overs, 3 maidens, 7 runs, 6 wickets and G. Hall finished with 5.1 overs, 3 maidens, 5 runs, 3 wickets. Hall was the first of a line of outstanding members from his family who contributed to the well being of the club both on and off the field for over 60 years.

The victims lost by an innings. Late in the season, Hall recorded analyses of 6 for 4 against Droxford, 6 for 15 versus Swanmore, and 4 for 7 when Soberton were overwhelmed: Hambledon 173-Soberton 30 and 44. In that match, W. Langridge recorded the first century for Hambledon since 1869. He and Atkins added 88 for the first wicket; Hall and Atkins each took four wickets in the Soberton first innings and Allen 6 for 16 in the second.

The season ended with a game against Mr. Alsen's XI in a continuation of the All-England festival. Jack Newman contributed a score of 80 and Mr. Extras 31 to Hambledon's 185, but the visitors passed this total comfortably and finished at 221 for 5.

An indication of the club's strengths and weaknesses around this time is given by the beautifully written averages for that season, in which the Hampshire players in the All-England match were included, not to the great advantage of all of them.

The committee felt, rightly, that their status had been enhanced as a result of the great occasion, and they demonstrated this in two ways. First in November 1908 they discussed leaving the Bishops Waltham league with a view to setting up a Hambledon and District League instead in which clubs within "6 miles or as may be decided" should be invited to participate. Subsequently they invited 11 clubs to join in competition for a cup which Captain Butler was to present. Hambledon's rivals and neighbours may have regarded these proposals as arrogant as there was a very poor response and early in 1909 the project was deferred, with the result that the club had to eat humble pie and they were fortunate to be invited to rejoin the Bishops Waltham League. However members' feathers were still ruffled when at the next general meeting the 22 who were present divided equally over that proposal which was passed only by the casting vote of Mr. Whalley-Tooker.

The second repercussion was the formation of a sub-committee to meet C.B. Fry who proposed that they arrange another major fixture on Broadhalfpenny Down but as already noted it did not come off. A third result was that from that time, the club used the emblem of the monument on its fixture card.

That spring, 1909, the name of Burton F.J. Cooper appears for the first time as a member of the committee. He was a dispensing chemist with a shop in the village, who became Hon Secretary in 1911 and whose association with the club lasted over 50 years. By the middle of June the club had lost five of the first eight games, largely due, as usual, to low scoring as they exceeded the century only twice: then, such is the unpredictability of cricket, they won six out of the next seven although they did not increase their run getting powers. An exception came when they defeated the Hants County Asylum at Knowle by 131 runs, Hambledon totalling 170 for six before declaring (W. Langridge 73 not out). In that match Vine took eight wickets for 20, figures nearly bettered by his wife, who recorded an analysis of 10 overs, 1 maiden, 18 runs, 6 wickets when the gentlemen beat the ladies by the narrow margin of 39 to 34. Unnerved, perhaps, by the result, the club went down to defeats in the last two matches with scores of just 46 and 21. The season's results showed eight wins and eight defeats from the programme of 16 games.

On and off the field, there was a squabble with the Assistant Secretary F.O. Edney, which arose from his letter published in the Hampshire Post on 18 June 1909, in reply to one which the paper had printed the previous week. He explained how he had stood as replacement umpire at the start of the match with the 20th Company R.G.A. in the temporary absence of T. Collis the club umpire, and his letter complained of the unsportsmanlike conduct of the club captain on the day, Mr. Allin, who, given out LBW by Edney, called Mr. Collis onto the field; Edney, supported by the visiting captain refused to leave the field and Collis much against his will had to retreat. After referring to the late start which happened because

Hambledon were not ready to take the field for three quarters of an hour after the due time of 11.30am Edney continued "The other point (in the letter to which he was replying) is that I lost the match by bad umpiring, and that was because I did not give out one of the visitors when he made two runs, and he afterwards got 52. Their contention is that he was run out, but I considered the man was in. It was said that I forgot to signal three wides, but nothing was said about the mistakes made last season with a certain umpire who was years older than I am. Why? Because he could afford to stand some of them drinks and I can't...whose was the fault that they lost again last Thursday, when playing Clanfield by over 60 runs? Was it the other umpire or bad captainship? The fact of the matter is they have lost a few matches this season, and I suppose someone or something must get the blame for it...your correspondent regards the postcard sent as a joke, but calling a player "a sneak" is not much of a joke. I don't know what would have been said if it had been sent to one of the clique, but I suppose that makes a difference if one plays in white or brown, although one pays the same subscription." He ended by mentioning that Mr. Whalley-Tooker was not in charge of the team on any of the relevant dates.

Apart from the personal criticism of the clubs Vice Captain, the letter contained enough adverse comment about Hambledon's cricket to raise the ire of the committee and at a general meeting on 23 June, from which the press were excluded (how often did they attend such meetings?), Edney was called upon to resign. He must have refused to do so as a motion to that effect was subsequently carried by ten votes to one, with eleven abstentions, which was just as much a criticism of Mr. Allin as it was of Edney. The meeting asked Mr. Whalley-Tooker to write to the Post "not to insert paragraphs detrimental to the club".

C.W. Knight took over as Assistant Secretary but the club found a willing replacement in Burton Cooper and soon the committee meetings were being held at his house.

There were some signs of a decline in interest in 1910; for example, in July a game had to be scratched as the club could not raise a team and at two general meetings in October, only seven and five members respectively were present. As many as nineteen however went to the meeting held on 21 January 1911 when Mr. Floud resigned as the Hon Secretary and Treasurer on leaving Hambledon, Burton Cooper succeeding him in both positions. There were also problems with the ground and in February the committee decided that the Captain should take care of it in consultation with the Hon Secretary/Treasurer.

We are now again without the results of matches, this time for 20 years, as although Mr. Cooper was an admirable administrator, and one of his first acts was to purchase a new scorebook, it and its successors up to 1930 are missing. It is clear that if there had been a slight lack of interest it had been resolved by 1912 when attendances at meetings rose up into the twenties, while at a general meeting held on 20 February 1913, when as many as 28 members were present, they agreed to institute a second eleven. In 1912, 24 members had played more than four innings: E. Whalley-Tooker topped the batting averages at the age of 50 (he still had 24 years of captaincy ahead of him!), and H. Turner was second. H.J. Allin scored most runs:-

	innings	not out	runs	average
E. Whalley-Tooker	10	1	165	18.33
H. Turner	10	3	117	16.71
H.J. Allin	16	0	226	14.12

Whalley-Tooker also headed the bowling averages with 22 wickets at 3.34, but the burden of the attack rested on G. Hall, 73 wickets for 341 runs, average 4.65 and G. Newland with 48 wickets for 282 runs, average 5.87. G. Hartridge was third in the batting and second in the bowling but he was not able to play very often. A typical eleven of that time was Whalley-Tooker, Turner, Allin, Newland, Cooper, G. Hall, G. Moon, H. Pink, C. Peggott, J. Hooker and F. Collis, J. Knight or H. Bucksey.

The side always carried a long tail only R. Newland with 105 runs, average 10 joining the first three in making any runs at all. Three members of the Bucksey family Richard, Fred and Harry played in 1912 and the family remained associated with the club for a very long period to come.

Captain Thomas Butler presided over a general meeting at which condolences were expressed to Mr. Whalley-Tooker on the death of his mother. Members present were informed that the 2nd XI had played eight games, and in addition what was described as a junior team had taken part in two. One of these may have been the match between the boys of Hambledon and Horndean, in which Hyde Charnock Whalley-Tooker, the son of Edward, dismissed nine of the opposition without conceding a single run: he bowled down six while three victims were caught or stumped by W. Langridge junior. Hambledon's 60 sufficed to defeat the crestfallen opposition who scored only seven and followed up with 41, by an innings. Apart from the two youngsters already named, Albert Hall, Jack Turner and Godfrey Parvin all had a prominent part to play in the future of the club.

CHAPTER 8

The season of 1914 began early with a game on Easter Monday, and ended prematurely. That season the team's results were played 18, won nine, lost seven, with one drawn game, and one tie. E. Whalley-Tooker headed the batting, but his average was only 14 for 117 runs, and G. Hall was again prominent in the bowling, capturing 38 wickets for only 132 runs.

The club minutes do not refer specifically to the outbreak of the First World War, but there are no meetings between the team selection committee on 14 August 1914 and a committee meeting on 17 March of the following year when Mr. Whalley-Tooker cleared the clubs deficit of £3.15. At the general meeting a fortnight later, when 14 members and two guests attended, they discussed the advisability of selecting officers for 1915, but adjourned without doing so and it was not until mid April that 13 members elected officers and resolved to carry on the club as usual for the duration of the war. As the war ground on for far longer than many people had anticipated, it came to dominate everything and only two meetings were held over the next four years, the first in May 1915 when it was unhappily reported that boys and youths, including some club members, had broken into the pavilion. A year later, in the depths of the hostilities, the club declined an invitation to play a match, but those present decided to redecorate the pavilion.

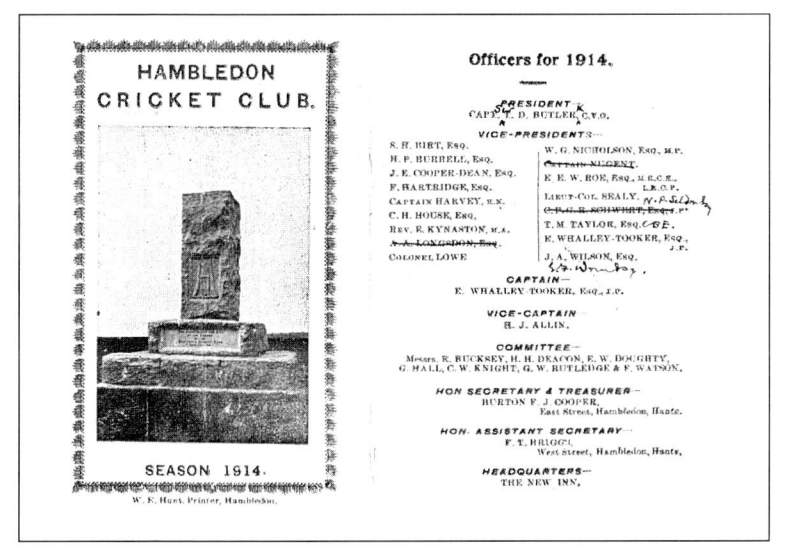

The fixture card for 1914

Then almost three years passed as the war dragged on, the male population were called up or volunteered, and year-by-year young men grew up and were called to arms. In Hambledon the sense of being on the front line may not have been as acute as it was in the 1939-45 war, but the naval activity in Portsmouth was only a forty minute bus ride away. As time went by there were many casualties from the village. Among the 33 dead commemorated on the war memorial are Arthur Edward Parvin, Stoker petty officer in HMS Bulwark who perished as early as 26 November 1914, J.W. Bucksey, and three members of the Hooker family who included in their ranks the groundsman at Brook Lane and other members of the team.

Sportsmen's day out. Hambledon Cricketers among the football team. October 1925. **At rear from left:** *G. Hall, 'Pug' Turner, H. Hooker.* **Far right:** *Mr. & Mrs. Stapeley and child.* **At front in charabanc:** *T. Smith, Jack Hall (in naval uniform), Burton F.T. Cooper (in trilby), L. May (bearded), F. Bucksey.* **Standing at front:** *J. Watson, Fred Hall, J. Knight, T. Parvin, G. Parvin, 'Punch' Hilary, Driver.*

CHAPTER 9

Starting Again

It is no surprise that Mr. Whalley-Tooker re-elected captain in 1915 and Burton F.J. Cooper were mainly responsible for the resuscitation of the club. Both were present at the war time meetings, such as they were, and little more than four months after the Armistice, on 4 March 1919 at The New Inn they met Messrs R. Bucksey, Hall and Rutledge (the landlord) and discussed the condition of the ground which was reported to be in good order, perhaps as the result of constant grazing by sheep, and agreed to undertake its rolling as soon as the necessary arrangements could be made - that is as soon as they could borrow a roller. The

Hyde Whalley-Tooker

attendance at the general meeting twelve days later must have exceeded their wildest expectations, indeed at 27 the number was almost equal to the largest gathering of members recorded up to that time and the names of the enthusiasts deserve to be recorded: E. Whalley-Tooker, in the chair, Dr. Roe, J.A. Wilson, H. Baker, V. Baker, and Messrs Bendall, Briggs, Brown, F.H. and R. Bucksey, T. Collis, F. and W.G. Dancaster, Deacon, Doughty, G. Hall, E. Hartridge, G. Parvin, Rutledge, L. and R. Newland, Sparshot, Alf and Jim Turner, W. Williams, H.C. Whalley-Tooker and E.F. Wren.

Hyde Whalley-Tooker was an enthusiastic cricketer as an adult, a medium paced bowler who went from Eton to Trinity Hall, Cambridge, and was for many years a law don then Senior Tutor and a Fellow of Downing College, Cambridge. Through his connections, a number of touring sides visited Hambledon from the late twenties onwards.

Sir Thomas Butler (he had been created a Knight Grand Cross of the Royal Victorian Order in 1918) was re-elected President, and Mr.

FIXTURES FOR SEASON 1919.

DATE.		NAME OF CLUB.	WHERE PLAYED	DAY OF WEEK.
May	17	Portsmouth Wesley	Home	Saturday
,,	29	E. Whalley-Tooker's XI.	Home	Thursday
June	9	Commercial Travellers, *Churcher's College*	Home *Home*	Monday *Thursday*
,,	12 21	Portsmouth Orleans	Home	Saturday
,,	28	Havant Rovers	Home	Saturday
July	5	Churcher's College	Away	Saturday
,,	12	Newtown Reading Room	Home	Saturday
,,	24	Price's School, Fareham	Away	Thursday
Aug.	2	~~Denmead~~		~~Saturday~~
,,	4	Droxford	Home	Monday
,,	9	Purbrook	Home	Saturday
,,	14	Swanmore	Away	Thursday
,,	16	Portsmouth Orleans	Home	Saturday
,,	21	East Meon	Away	Thursday
,,	23	Portsmouth Wesley	Home	Saturday
,,	28	~~Newtown Reading Room~~	~~Home~~	~~Thursday~~
,,	30	Purbrook	Away	Saturday
Sept.	4	~~East Meon~~	~~Home~~	~~Thursday~~
,,	6	~~Havant Rovers~~	~~Home~~	~~Saturday~~
,,	11	~~Admiral Bayley's XI.~~ *E. Meon*	Home	Thursday
,,	13 18	~~Swanmore~~ *E.W. Jonkers XI* *St. Clark's XI*	Home *Home*	Saturday *Thursday*

Whalley-Tooker as captain, with H.C. Brown his vice, while Cooper continued as hon. secretary. There was at this initial meeting at least some relaxation of the previous jealously guarded right of membership, for Mr. Cooper announced that in view of the long interval since the last general meeting everyone present should have a vote. In March the equipment was found to be in satisfactory condition, and sufficient in quantity for the early part of the season, but balls and batting gloves would be required later on. During March and April Mr. Cooper worked hard to rebuild the fixture list. An inflationary period set in after the war and there was a good deal of unemployment as the heroes returned to their homes while those who returned to their jobs found that their pre-war salaries were inadequate. The effect as far as the cricket club was concerned was that discussions about the provision of tea went on over several meetings, before the hon. secretary declared that it was quite possible to provide tea at one shilling (5p) a head, and he must have felt more than justified when the club made a profit of £0.10.0 (50p) on the first match, at which Mrs. Withers and Mrs. Deacon were responsible for the refreshments. Fixtures continued to be made on through June, most of them on early closing day which was Thursday. The civilians were to play the services, and the first eleven the next 22. In August Whalley-Tooker transported an under 16 team to play Captain Coleridge's XI at Corhampton. The season was successful and enjoyable. It is a pity that there is not a surviving scorebook but we can gain some idea of the club's progress from the annual reports which Mr. Cooper gave to general meetings. He told the general meeting on 15 December 1919 that the club had played 19 matches, which was a little less than those arranged before the war, of which they won as many as 14 games and lost only five, an unrivalled degree of success. Runs were always hard to get as Hambledon averaged 7.54 runs per wicket as against opponents 5.53. Godfrey Parvin an outstanding young player who was also well known locally as a goalkeeper headed the batting and Hyde Whalley-Tooker captured 49 wickets at just under four runs apiece. Lady Butler, the President's wife, offered a handsome silver gilt cup as a trophy for annual competition, and the meeting, while agreeing that rules be drawn up for its future presentation agreed that the first recipient should be "the esteemed captain", now in his 57th year, whose name was duly engraved on the cup.

Attendances at general meetings continued to be good: there were 24 at the spring 1920 meeting, and elections for the committee were usually keenly contested, but President, captain, and the hon. secretary/treasurer were never opposed. In May 1920 the committee prepared for the first grand match since the war, arranged as an all day fixture with the Royal Naval School of Music, with lunch at two shillings (10p) a head, while the Hambledon brass band played on the ground. For travel to ordinary away matches club members would pay nine pence each (about 4p), but if there was room for non-members they would have to contribute 1/6d (or 7.5 pence). Alas, there were no carriers available on those figures: Messrs Chase offered 16 shillings (80p) for a single horse bus, or 25 shillings (£1.25) for one drawn by a pair. Mr. Batchelor of Worlds End tendered 12 shillings (60 pence) per match for a single horse conveyance carrying seven players. Perhaps by 1920 four of the team could provide their own transport? Certainly motorised public transport served Hambledon during the First World War so some opponents were accessible by bus, as well as by horse drawn vehicles.

That August the club played opponents who were to become the regular users of Broadhalfpenny Down, Messrs Wadham Bros the motor dealers. This year for the first time the club minutes deplore the adverse effect on team selection of the football season.

The season's results and leading scorers and wicket takers were carefully noted by Mr. Cooper:

For 1920,   played 24, won 11,   lost 11,   drawn 2
2nd XI   4,   2,   2

Godfrey Parvin was first in batting and he won the Butler Cup. C. May was top of the bowling.

The accounts showed a small balance in hand but there was a deficit on the tea account because of the clubs purchase of cups and saucers and a copper. An honorarium was paid to Mrs. Wilkins and Mrs. Deacon for preparing the teas.

For 1921, played 24, won 12, lost 11, drawn 1

A. Moon was first in batting with 140 runs, average 15, and A. Amos finished top of the bowling, capturing 34 wickets for 172 runs. There were no nominations for the Butler Cup and after a pause the meeting adopted Mr. Whalley-Tooker's nomination of G. Parvin.
A working profit of a pound or so on the season was augmented by a favourable balance of £7.9.10 on the teas. The captain continued in office for the 27th season.

For 1922 there were signs in a decline in strength. The AGM that winter was attended by only seven members who heard that of 23 matches played no more than six were one as against 14 lost. Godfrey Parvin again won the Butler Cup. The meeting discussed at some length the need for more members under 18 years of age, and the need for practice facilities and systematic coaching to attract boys to the club. J. Knight and Edward Whalley-Tooker agreed to deal with the problem and undertake the coaching.

We get a glimpse of the club's cricket at that time from a letter written sixty years later by Chris Turner the uncle of Topsy and a member of one of the families which have for a long time been involved with Hambledon cricket: "It was in 1922 I first played for Hambledon and started working on the ground....and going to away matches in a horse-drawn conveyance, and fielding in long grass at home games where sheep fed in the outfield." The work on the ground and the long grass in the outfield remained problems for members for many

CHAPTER 9

Officers for 1925.

PRESIDENT—
CAPT. SIR T. D. BUTLER, K.C.V.O.

VICE-PRESIDENTS—

W. BUCKSEY, Esq.
N. F. DRUCE, Esq.
F. HARTRIDGE, Esq.
C. H. HOUSE, Esq.
COL. KEOGH.
REV. E. KYNASTON, M.A.
COL. LOWE.
CAPT. MORGAN.

W. G. NICHOLSON, Esq., M.P.
MAJOR RUNDLE.
LIEUT. COL. SEALY.
T. M. TAYLOR, Esq., C.B.E.
E. WHALLEY-TOOKER, Esq., J.P.
THE MISSES WILSON.
E. F. WREN, Esq.
MRS. WREN.

Dr. C. H. ROCK.

CAPTAIN—
E. WHALLEY-TOOKER, Esq., J.P.

VICE-CAPTAIN—
G. HALL.

COMMITTEE—
Messrs. R. BUCKSEY, E. W. DOUGHTY, A. HALL,
G. KNIGHT, F. MACEY, E. PARVIN & G. PARVIN.

HON. SECRETARY—
BURTON F. J. COOPER,
East Street, Hambledon, Hants.

HON. TREASURER—
E. F. WREN,
The Court House, Hambledon, Hants.

HEADQUARTERS—
THE NEW INN.

HAMBLEDON CRICKET CLUB.

SEASON 1925.

HAMBLEDON C.C.
LIST OF FIXTURES.

Date		Day.	Name of Club.	Where Played	Match Scores.	Own Scores.	Result.
May	2	Saturday	Wadham's	Home			
,,	9	,,	6th Hants Regt.	Home			
,,	16	,,	Portsmouth Brotherhood	Home			
,,	23	,,	Purbrook	Home			
,,	30	,,	North Stoneham	Away			
June	1	Monday (all day)	Portsmouth Wesley	Home			
,,	4	Thursday	East Meon	Home			
,,	6	Saturday	Red Company	Home			
,,	13	,,	Wadham's	Home			
,,	18	Thursday	Hants Mental Hospital	Away			
,,	20	Saturday	North Stoneham	Home			
,,	27	,,	6th Hants Regt.	Home			
July	4	,,	Engineers Sports	Home			
,,	11	,,	Winchester College	Broad Halfpen'y			
,,	16	Thursday	Droxford	Home			
,,	18	Saturday	Havant Rovers	Home			
,,	25	,,	Portsmouth Brotherhood	Home			
August	1	,,	Portsmouth Trinidad	Home			
,,	3	Monday (all day)	Caledonian Athletic	Home			
,,	6	Thursday	Hants County Asylum	Away			
,,	8	Saturday	Purbrook	Away			
,,	13	Thursday	Signal School (R.N.B.)	Home			
,,	15	Saturday	Red Company	Home			
,,	20	Thursday	Droxford	Away			
,,	22	Saturday	Portsmouth Wesley	Home			
,,	27	Thursday	East Meon	Away			
,,	29	Saturday	Signal School Civilian Sports	Home			

Fixture card for 1925.

– 73 –

years to come. Teas were by far the greatest contributor to a working profit of £11 or so.

In 1923 the results were even worse with only seven victories as against 16 defeats with three drawn matches out of the 26 played and the statistics tell their own story:

> For Hambledon 2041 runs for 297 wickets, average 6.87.
> Against   2418 runs for 264 wickets, average 9.15.

Godfrey Parvin headed the batting but he was not at his best, scoring only 206 runs at an average of 12 and the bowling of F. Macey, whose 51 wickets cost 5.54 runs each was not enough to counteract the weakness of the batting but he deservedly was awarded the Butler Cup.

In February 1924 a large ant heap formed on the ground and the hon. secretary was instructed to find a suitable man to level it. No doubt Mr. Cooper, a man of resource, was equal to the task. As a chemist he may have resolved the problem himself.

The results were marginally better in 1924 when victories equalled losses at 13. Not a single match was drawn. Runs per wicket for the club, 5.50, were nearer to the opponents' average of 6.71. The diminutive Fred Hall, a builder and a familiar and successful figure from this period on for nearly 40 years, and a future captain of the club, was awarded the Butler Cup for his all-round play, although he headed neither the batting nor the bowling. The next season, 1925, was no more successful than its predecessors. W. Langridge headed the batting with 198 runs in six innings and Hall, playing more regularly averaged 12 for his 323 runs. Whalley-Tooker at the age of 61 was top of the bowling, his 26 wickets costing a littler over three runs a piece but the Butler Cup went to Parvin whose victims totalled 99 at 5.02 runs each and he again won the trophy in 1926.

Other events of those post war years up to the resignation of B.F.J. Cooper included the committee's decision in 1922 that they did not have the legal right to grant the use of the cricket ground to teams coming from outside the parish, an understanding which remained intact as long as the club were only the tenants. Even when Mr. Cooper himself asked for the use of the ground by the Pharmaceutical Association, there was such a prolonged discussion in committee that he withdrew the proposal and agreed to investigate afresh what the conditions of tenure were. In June 1922 he and Mr. Whalley-Tooker reported back reminding the committee of the limitation of use of Brook Lane for "The exercise and recreation for the inhabitants of the said parish, and the neighbourhood". When a year later a resident of Denmead applied for membership of the club, his application was refused although Denmead was a part of the civil parish of Hambledon and remained so until 1932.

Almost every spring now there was difficulty in fixing the team's transport to away matches while Messrs Chase from Hambledon and Batchelor from Worlds End slowly submitted their competing tenders. In 1922 it took until 6 June to sort it out and even then Mr.G. Chase had to attend before the committee in person to agree the figure of £1 per journey and the following year it took until the end of May. At the end of the season the committee expressed dissatisfaction with the service on at least two occasions. When the conveyance was motorised is not clear.

The "newly formed Broadhalfpenny Cricket Club" receives a mention in the minutes in March 1924 - but what was it? That year Winchester College purchased the old ground and many more acres and this marked the start of a new life for cricket on the Down with the first big match of the new era taking place in 1925, but when Winchester College had renewed the ground and regular play resumed there Messrs Wadham brothers were the home side. Perhaps the Broadhalfpenny CC was a bright idea which did not get onto the ground, let alone off it. So for some reason or reasons unknown Hambledon missed the opportunity of a return to Broadhalfpenny which led to a good deal of spasmodic discussion over the next 40 years.

Meanwhile they contemplated improvements at Brook Lane: works to provide accommodation for ladies and enlargement of the shed to provide more room for the lawn mowers. The total estimate of a little below £5 or the equivalent of £100 today was rejected by the committee by seven votes to two, a rare revolt against Messrs Whalley-Tooker and Cooper who had recommended its acceptance.

*The Hambledon Team against Winchester College, 23 July 1925.
Back row: W.J Arnold, P.M.Hall, F.J.B. Cooper, E. Whalley-Tooker,
H.C. McDonnell and A.D. Bonham-Carter.
Front row; A.E. Knight, H.S. Altham, E.R. Wilson, G. Parvin,
F. Hall and C.T. Ashton.*

Chapter 10
Back In The Public Eye

By March 1925 arrangements were underway for Hambledon, as visitors, to play again on Broadhalfpenny Down. Ashley Mote indicates that the impetus came from Harry Altham, the cricket historian and Winchester College master who had also been a practical cricketer for Repton School, Surrey and Hampshire. The match against Winchester College fixed for 23 July was the most publicised one in which the village had been involved since the All-England game of 1908. The timing was significant for just as the unveiling of the monument had been proceeded by the publication by E.V. Lucas of The Hambledon Men, in which he had gathered together in one volume the earlier writings on the club, so the precursor of the 1925 game was the Hambledon Cricket Chronicle in which the club's surviving minutes and accounts up to 1796 were published with scholarly commentary by Frederick Samuel Ashley-Cooper. He had built up a high profile as a cricket researcher and historian over the previous 25 years and Altham was careful to invite him to the match at which he diligently recorded the scores. The match against Winchester College coming at a time when interest in Hambledon's past was again being rekindled attracted enormous interest and a large crowd saw a two innings a side match completed in one day.

The College XI included a number of young men destined to play first class cricket. Patrick Kingsley, a future Oxford blue and a prominent batsman in the late 1920s before he began a career with the Duchy of Lancaster, which culminated in his appointment as clerk and the award of a knighthood, was probably the most distinguished. However A.W. Richardson also had a claim to fame as captain of Derbyshire from 1931 to 1936, when they won the County Championship for the only time. A.M. Tew was a future Oxford cricket blue. Much interest centred on the two cousins appearing on opposing sides: A.D. Bonham Carter for Winchester, and Major A. Bonham Carter for Hambledon. Each excelled, the schoolboy scoring 85 and 28, and the Major 56 for the village.

Hambledon were fortified by the presence of Altham, Rockley Wilson of Yorkshire and England, who was also a master at the College, and A.E. Knight the Leicestershire and England professional batsman, who is said to have prayed, devoutly and audibly and usually with success before he faced each ball. Two further first class cricketers in the side were H.C. McDonell of Twyford School, a highly successful slow bowler for Cambridge and Surrey before joining Hampshire and C.T. Ashton of Essex, one of the three brothers who in succession each captained Winchester and Cambridge.

Godfrey Parvin, Fred Hall, Burton Cooper and E. Whalley-Tooker formed the Hambledon component with P.M. Hall a Hampshire player and local estate agent, and W.J. Arnold, land agent, making up their 12. Wilson and Ashton took most of the College wickets, but Parvin had three cheap victims and shared in an opening stand of 39 with Altham. The special correspondent of The Observer wrote, "You might have thought it was derby day on this remote Down. Even when the match was over, the lonely roads were dangerous with cars, cycles and straggling pedestrians of all ages. A double and treble rank of motorcars and brakes surrounded the ground...Winchester were beaten by a quarter to four, but still the people gathered on the Down. The big marquees were well patronised. Hilarity issued from the parlour of The Bat and Ball. Hambledon village finds the spot too remote...the neat ground and dapper pavilion of the club are put outside the village." The Wykehamist noted that many famous figures were seen on the ground, and the importance of the occasion was "Very widely recognised." Yet at the end of the season (which was a poorish one as indicated at Chapter Nine above,) the balance sheet showed cash in hand of only about £4, plus a catering profit of £8 or so.

They repeated the fixture on 11 July 1927, but although H.C. McDonnell and A.J.L. Hill, who had been an outstanding bat for Hampshire for 15 years before the First World War, and had represented England in Tests against South Africa in 1895-96, played for Hambledon, the home side were dismissed for only 46. Worse still the start of the game was ruined by torrential rain. Even on such a day, about 500 members of the public took the trouble to turn up. A third game was played two years later when the College's total of 162 gave them victory by five runs.

Over the next few years thanks to Hyde Whalley-Tooker, the village played three matches against Downing College: in the first in 1929 Hambledon, who were strengthened by the presence of W.G. Lowndes, the future Hampshire captain, R.C. Robertson-Glasgow, the Somerset bowler and writer, and two well known military players, Major W.A. Trasenster, and Captain A.F. Coryton, put up a good reply to Downing's total of 223, but it was two local players, Fred Hall, 81 not out, and Horace Clark, 39, who saved the day, Hall playing one of his finest innings which made up nearly half of his sides total of 168 for seven wickets. Each side achieved victory once when the fixture was repeated in 1930 and 1931. In another game resulting from the Hyde Whalley-Tooker connection, involving Eton Ramblers in 1930, Hambledon amassed 238, E.C. Lee (the Hampshire County player around the end of the XIX Century) making 72, W. Langridge 43 and Jack Turner 33, to which the Ramblers responded with 111 for six.

On 26 March 1926 the general meeting re-elected Mr. Whalley-Tooker captain for the 32nd successive year: Burton Cooper resigned as hon. secretary as he was leaving Hambledon (he had given up as hon. treasurer in 1922). He was deservedly elected as Permanent Honorary Vice President and was the recipient of a framed testimonial. He moved to Kent, presumably on retirement from his profession, and lived on into the 1960s.

His successor was the successful bowler and village blacksmith F. Macey. The hon. treasurer E.F. Wren also resigned because of prolonged illness and A. Hall was elected in his place. In July occurred the death of F. Rutledge landlord of The New Inn and another long-standing supporter of the club. That season, 1926, was the most successful for some years, victories exceeding defeats by 17 to 13; draws as ever were a rare occurrence and there was only one. The Butler Cup yet again went to Godfrey Parvin. The club offered additional remuneration to Mrs. Withers for her excellent service in the provision of teas but in spite of the increased payment she did not continue and early in 1927 the committee had to ask Mrs. Apps to take over the catering. Happy events that year, the presentation to Sir Thomas and Lady Butler on their Golden Wedding, and the election of Commander E.P. Goldsmith as a Vice President, were followed by a mystery which arose after an away match with Petersfield at the beginning of August. A Mr. Sadler wrote that following happenings by certain members of the visiting team on August Bank Holiday, his house had been ignored...and he was not inclined to allow any room to be used for any future meetings. Had Hambledon come late and rowdy to a function at a Petersfield pub? The Hambledon committee was ordered to apologise to the home side about their trouble and expense.

During the years on either side of the First World War there was a switch in the pattern of fixtures played by the club: in 1911, of the 21 matches arranged, 16 were on Thursdays, early closing day, three on Bank Holiday Mondays and only two on Saturdays but by 1919 ten out of 19 were played on Saturdays and seven years after that, of an increased programme of 30 games, 20 were played on Saturdays and only seven on Thursdays, with a few Bank Holiday fixtures, and this arrangement set the pattern for the future. In one respect results still differed from those of later years before league cricket arose - draws were a rarity: in 1927 of 30 matches played, 16 were won and all the remainder lost.

Godfrey Parvin scored most runs, 244 at 15.4 runs an innings and he took 62 wickets average 5, but the hon. secretary F. Macey was awarded the Butler Cup. The club's finances were steady thanks to the in-house catering, the balance in the clubs favour being nearly £19 at the end of the long, hot summer of 1928. That year results showed a great improvement with 16 wins quite outshining nine losses but there were as many as five drawn games. The Butler Cup found a new destination in A. Newland and Captain Hinde topped the bowling averages.

Edward Whalley-Tooker, and his brother Hyde, master of Foxhounds, on 1 January 1929.

Features of the next few years were the laying on of a water supply from "the trough in the meadow" to the pavilion and players and caterers must soon have wondered how they had ever managed without it. Familiar names appearing for the first time were Tichborne Park in the fixture list, and Chris Turner was winner of the Butler Cup in 1929.

Then there was the mid winter game played on New Years Day 1929 against the Invalids: this was not strictly a Hambledon fixture as the home side were described as the Hampshire Eskimos. Their opponents were a well-established touring side of literary and other personalities raised by the poet and editor J.C. (later Sir John) Squire. The opening of the match, described as a humorous protest against the encroachment of football on the cricket season, coincided with the meet of the Hambledon Hunt at The Bat and Ball. The occasion brought yet another large crowd to Broadhalfpenny Down and an

CHAPTER 10

Above: First January 1929, the Hambledon Hunt, master Hyde Whalley-Tooker, rides by the pitch on Broadhalfpenny Down where his brother is captain of the fielding side.

Hampshire Eskimoes v The Invalids, 1st January 1929.

army of press photographers and "kinematograph operators" captured the scene. In addition to Edward Whalley-Tooker, included in the home team were R. Bucksey, Macey and Godfrey Parvin from Hambledon while the visiting team was full of famous names of the time including R. Straus the novelist, B.W. O'Donnell, conductor of the BBC military band, A.B. Peters the literary agent, A.G. Macdonell author of "England Their England" the most famous collection of witty stories of the time, and Walter Monckton, a former Harrow wicket keeper, who was to be a leading figure in the abdication of Edward VIII, and later still a cabinet minister. Well known now as the writer of the carol Bethlehem Down and other poems set to music by Peter Warlock (Philip Heseltine) is another member of the Eskimos Bruce Blunt, who liked his drink and was an inhabitant of Bramdean when his journalistic duties in London allowed.

The Hambledon brass band was in attendance throughout the match and among the pieces they played was the Cricketers of Hambledon, a product of the Peter Warlock/Bruce Blunt combination.

The brilliant play of Horace Clark was the outstanding feature of the match, once the Hunt had departed. Lunch was taken between the innings but as one of the papers recorded: "There were no elaborate preparations for the meal, the only food available being bread and cheese and pickles, and the house was so besieged that it was difficult to secure even these". The Bat and Ball was much better provisioned by Dick Orders when the millennium was celebrated on 31 December 1999 and 1 January 2000!

Mr. Macey was re-elected secretary for 1931, but only after a vote - eleven to three in his favour, in the first ever recorded contest for the post. The years 1930 and 1931 were busy ones for the club and the secretary. The club approached Winchester College about their wish to mow out a larger square and they gladly accepted Captain Goldsmith's offer of a motor mower. The Captain was also the prime mover in arranging another important match for the club against his ship, the land base HMS Nelson, to be played in XVIII Century dress.

Amidst these pre-occupations, at the general meeting on 1 April 1931, the hon. secretary was absent, and J.E. Turner was elected in his place. When the committee convened on the following day, Mr. Turner had to report that he had received no details of fixtures whatever from the late hon. secretary: apparently nothing had been arranged. Mr. Turner, as in many years to come, was equal to the crisis. He bought a new scorebook and it records a continuity of fixtures from 13 June onwards, all of which he had arranged by the 15 April! Of these 15 resulted in victory, 14 were lost, and only one match which was started was drawn because of the weather. There must however have been others that were rained off in what was the first of two deplorably wet summers (I am writing this in the middle of 2000!). The weather in turn accounts for the very low scoring in 1931. Hambledon exceeded three figures on only four occasions that year: their opponents fared

CHAPTER 10

J.E Turner (left) and Chris Turner

no worse, but this was largely due to HMS Nelson who achieved this target twice in one day, when Hambledon's match against them came off on 1 August. The Hambledon team, wearing top hats, vest-waistcoats, knee breeches, silk stockings and buckled shoes assembled by The George Inn and when the visiting side clad in tarpaulin hats, checked shirts and striped trousers, and wearing pig tails, entered the village, E. Whalley-Tooker advanced and challenged them to a match at cricket. Lieutenant R.T. (Dick) White had the greatest pleasure in accepting the challenge, which as the son of a former Yorkshire cricket captain, Sir Archibald White, he was well qualified to do.

Three cheers for the Navy! Hambledon greet their opponents HMS Nelson. Edward Whalley-Tooker left of centre, Fred Hall to left of him, Stumps Turner third from right.

The match was played under what were believed to be the same conditions as in the days of Richard Nyren, 150 years before. The wicket consisted of two stumps with a "stumping hole" between them into which the ball had to be placed at some danger to the fielder receiving the ball, to run the batsman out. To save himself, he had to place his bat in the hole. On occasion, hand and bat would arrive together! The creases were scratched in the turf, and the runs were "notched" on a stick with a jack-knife by H. (Stumps) Turner just as, it was said, he had done as a boy, 45 years before (although Hambledon had been using scorebooks long before that.)

By 3pm there were 3,000 spectators on Broadhalfpenny Down. The scoreboard was manned by Rudevic May who wore a smock and had with him a large umbrella which, he claimed, had been used to shelter the team from the rain 150 years before.

HMS Nelson won by 63 notches. There was only one guest in the Hambledon team, Major Bonham Carter of 1925 fame. Otherwise the score sheet shows a typical team of the period

H.M.S. NELSON

First Innings	Second Innings
Major J.M. Tuke, c. Bucksey, b. Newland ... 6	— c. Hooker, b. Macey 2
Lieutenant-Comander J.W. Farquhar, ...	
b. Newland 12	— b. Newland 5
Lieutenant R.T. White, c. Bucksey, ...	— c. Whalley-Tooker
,b. Newland 11	— b. Langridge 39
Lieutenant-Commander	
E.S. Satterthwaite, b. Turner 31	— c. Hooker, b.Langridge 69
Paymaster-Midshipman J.E. Stevens, ...	
c. Doughty, b. Macey 0	— c. Hooker, b. Hall 12
Lieutenant-Commander	
G.W.G.Simpson, b. Newland 5	— not out 51
Captain F.B. Watson, c. Bucksey, b. Hall 5	— b. Macey 11
Commander J.S. Cowie, b. Langridge 21	— b. Macey 12
Paymaster-Lieut E.A. May, c. & b. Hall 5	— c. Whalley-Tooker b. Hall, ... 0
Sub-Lieut N.J.W. Barttelot, b. Hall 1	— c. Langridge, b.Whalley-Tooker ..12
Midshipman M.A.L. Cooper, not out 5	not out 18

Total   102   *231

* Innings declared closed

HAMBLEDON

First Innings	Second Innings
W. Langridge, c. Satterthwaite, b. Stevens 0	— b. Stevens 4
F. Hall, b. Satterthwaite 8	— c. & b. White 25
R. Bucksey, c. Barttelot, b. Stevens 7	— c. Barttelot, b.White 6
Major A. Bonham Carter, c. Cooper	
b. Satterthwaite 12	— b. Satterthwaite 3
C. Turner, c. & b. Satterthwaite 8	— b. Satterthwaite 30
F.G. Macey, c. May, b. Stevens 22	— c. Barttelot, b.White 4
W.A. Newland, c. Barttelot,	
b. Satterthwaite 34	— not out 43
H. Hooker, c. Stevens, b. Satterthwaite 12	— c. Satterthwaite, b. White 5
Paymaster-Captain E.P. Goldsmith,	
b. Satterthwiate 19	— c. Cooper, b. White 5
E.W. Doughty, not out 10	— c. White, b.Satterthwaite 0
E. Whalley-Tooker, c. Barttelot,	
b. Satterthwaite 6	— c. Tuke, b. Satterthwaite 7

Tota   138   132

After the crowd had enjoyed the match and the numerous side shows around the ground, Admiral Sir H.M. Hodges auctioned the work of Turner: that is the notched sticks of the scorer and not the artwork of the painter. The Royal Marine Band played on what The Times described as the village green, and dancing by children around the Maypole, a bonfire and fireworks concluded the festival.

The whole event was the brainchild of Captain Goldsmith. One of his tasks was to reassure F.S. Ashley-Cooper about the details of the antiquarian nature of the match. On 4 July 1931 he wrote to justify the inclusion of two stump wickets, and tall hats worn by the Hambledon team: there was no intention of playing in smock frocks...he was sorry that Ashley Cooper could have thought him guilty of such vandalism. In reality by 1781, 150 years before, three stump wickets were in use: the dress of the naval team seems more appropriate to the 1820s or 30s. The fact is that Captain Goldsmith's intention was to rekindle enthusiasm in the village. That year he had also arranged in the spring for the fixture cards and balance sheet to be printed and had acted as a true benefactor to the club when the committee were having difficulty in raising teams and had thought it necessary to reduce the subscription for juniors to a shilling (5p).

It was largely due to his efforts that receipts exceeded expenditure by £18 that season.

Fred Hall twice exceeded 50 in August, scoring 60 against Southsea Wanderers, and 75 in the game with Swanmore a week later. In such a damp summer the bowlers naturally prospered, C. Turner, Newland, A. Gibson and Hall constantly returning remarkable figures, while Macey returned to the fold to complete a formidable attack. When Hambledon's score of 24 sufficed for victory by three runs over North Stoneham, Newland's figures were 8.3 overs, 5 maidens, 6 wickets for 8 runs. Macey took 9 for 18 against

A member of the HMS Nelson team, 1931

Stedham and 8 for 19 against North End Business Men, while Hyde Whalley-Tooker seized the opportunity to capture 6 Swanmore victims for 7 runs. Fred Hall won the batting cup with the best figures achieved for the club for many years, 538 runs at an average of 19.

The committee did not want a repetition of the problem with the secretary in the previous spring: the general meeting on 19 November resolved that in future the hon. secretary should be elected at the general meeting at the end of each season rather than wait for the spring meeting. The following spring they re-elected E. Whalley-Tooker captain for the 37th time. G. Hall was elected vice captain. Through some local connection a long distance away match was arranged with Croydon Cable Works and it was decided that reinforcements should be called up, the names suggested including R.C. Robertson-Glasgow, and W.G. Lowndes. To prepare perhaps for a return visit, a ladies lavatory was installed at Ridge Meadow at a cost of a little under £3. Although not so successful financially 1932 brought better results than for some years past, victories exceeding defeats by 18 to 11. The pavilion was refurbished, and the team pictures and the club flag were transferred from The New Inn. Thanks to the efforts of Col Lewis, and F. Bucksey, who hired horse and machiery for the purpose, the ground was also improved.

The season featured more outstanding analyses by what had become a formidable attack. Croydon Cable Works gave the club a good hiding, bowling them out twice for 33, while themselves scoring 106. Fred Hall's best performance occurred in the match against Knowle Hospital in June. After A. Newland had returned the admirable figures of 6 for 61 in the opposition's total of 187, Hall hit up 133, monopolising the scoring to such an extent that when he was eighth out the total was only 175. With Dr. Horn (five) he put on 95 for the eighth wicket. His figures, 828 runs at an average of 27 were the best ever for the club up to that date and he naturally won the Butler Cup. There was a close fight between A. Newland, 90 wickets average 7 and Chris Turner 94 at 8 runs each for honours with the ball.

Colonel Lewis was elected vice captain after a ballot at the general meeting on 8 March 1933 and Chris Turner replaced H. Hooker as groundsman as the latter was unable to continue with the job. As skipper Mr. Whalley-Tooker at the age of 71 was beginning to ease off, and when Colonel Lewis resigned in the following spring Turner took over as vice captain. In 1933 he captured 124 wickets at an average cost of 9 but Fred Hall still earned the Butler Cup with 946 runs at an average of 25 and 106 wickets at just under 10 each.

At the spring meeting in 1934 H (Stumps) Turner the one legged scorer resigned after 48 years service, which, if not rivalling Sir Thomas Butler's tenure as President exceeded Whalley-Tookers turn in office by some 7 years. It is quite a thought that he scored almost every match up to 1933 and that without him this book could not have been written. The committee were left to decide on a testimonial for him, and to find a successor.

Edward Whalley-Tooker, Captain 1896 to 1936, President 1937 - 1940 and his wife Dorothy, President 1940 - 1962.

CHAPTER 11

After Whalley-Tooker

In 1933 and 1934, Mr. Turner widened the fixture list by the addition of such opponents as Eton College Servants, Portsmouth Amateurs and well known touring sides such as the Nondescripts (their total 201: Hambledon 56 and 56 for 6) and the Frogs who scored 136 for seven to which Hambledon replied with 48 and 125 for eight. The village drew with Croydon Cable Works at Croydon in June thanks to Chris Turner and Fred Hall. In the home team's total of 168, Turner had the notable analysis of 27 overs, 11 maidens, 55 runs and 8 wickets, and his score of 21 provided support for Hall who made 64 as Hambledon survived at 129 for eight. Three weeks later the club played a very odd match with Southwick. After Hambledon were put out for 95, to which F. Banting contributed 26 made up entirely of boundaries - 46664, Southwick put together a total of 193. Their second wicket took the score past Hambledon's total but the match then took an unusual turn as the second wicket batsmen batted on and on to add 177 together against a varied selection of bowlers: after the stand was broken two other batsmen retired before six wickets fell for seven runs.

In the face of the increasingly strong opposition it is not really surprising that in 1934 defeats comfortably outnumbered victories by 20 to 13. But there was a handsome profit on the year's work, and away matches at Croydon and Winchester College added considerably to the season's interest. F. Hall again received the Butler Cup as a reward for his 761 runs, 74 wickets, and 33 catches, but Turner had the better bowling figures with 115 wickets at just under 10 each. The testimonial for Stumps Turner produced £8.75, which is the equal of £260 in today's money and was presented to him, together with a framed list of the subscribers by Mr. Whalley-Tooker at the general meeting in November 1934.

The next year began on a note of great sadness with the death of Commander E.P. Goldsmith, that good friend of the club. Mr. Whalley-Tooker who presided over a general meeting with an attendance of 23 was re-elected captain. Money was to be spent on both the cricket square and the outfield and on painting the pavilion. In this busy season of 31 fixtures the names of Hall and Turner were again dominant but other names coming into the picture were G. Hartridge, who made a number of useful scores, J. Bourne and J. Watson. The shock of dismissal by East Meon for 16, by

Southwick for 34 and by the masters of Portsmouth Grammar School for 19, all in June, was a little offset later in the season, when the club amassed 176 against Southsea Wanderers, Chris Turner top scoring with 42, which led to an innings victory, and followed this with 237 against those formidable old opponents Knowle Hospital. G. Hartridge, 75, and D. Miller added 111 and H. Hooker with 48 and Harrison, 31, contributed useful scores. Turner and Hartridge then shared the wickets in the dismissal of the Hospital for 160. When Whalley-Tooker's side played Mrs. Goldsmith's side in a memorial game in August, N. Fiennes who is now Lord Saye and Seale contributed 101 not out to Whalley-Tookers total of 125: he and O. Fiennes, who made only three added 62 for the ninth wicket. They are both grandsons of Sir Thomas Butler.

There was only one nominee for the Butler Cup: he scored 551 runs and captured 89 wickets and his name was Fred Hall. Chris Turner was ahead of him in the bowling with 90 wickets.

A change in the generalship of the club was imminent. Mr. Whalley-Tooker was approaching the age of 74 and at the general meeting on 13 March 1936 he indicated that he was unable to continue: he had long since ceased to make runs. The membership actually implored him to stay on and he agreed although in the event he played very little. The season was not successful as 11 successes were counterbalanced by as many as 18 defeats. Hall began the season with a series of good performances with bat and ball and at the beginning of June J. Smith returned figures of five for 27, seven for 70 and seven for 43. Later Chris Turner's analyses in consecutive innings were five for 22, seven for 22, seven for 55, six for 29, and then on 16 July he, with Smith shattered Croydon Cable Works whom they dismissed for 21, obtaining the following figures:

Turner	10 overs,	7 maidens,	3 runs,	5 wickets
Smith	9.5 overs,	2 maidens,	18 runs,	5 wickets

Yet although Turner finished the season with five for 52 against Portchester, and eight for 17 including the hat trick against the City of Portsmouth, Hambledon simply could not get enough runs for consistent success, mustering, in what was admittedly a wettish summer, no more than five totals of 100 during the whole season. The highest batting average was only 19 achieved by R. Harrison who played only 9 innings. Smith took 46 wickets at an average of just over 7, while Turner captured 95 at slightly greater cost. Hall however again took the Butler Cup for his service with both bat and ball.

CHAPTER 11

The general meeting on 5 March 1937 saw the final, and even at his advanced age, unwanted retirement from the captaincy of Mr. Whalley-Tooker: although 20 members attended that meeting, he did not, an event by itself. He wrote to indicate his "strong inclination to resign in the interest of the club." Amid many expressions of sadness, the proposition was made to appoint him as consultative captain and this was greeted with applause and carried unanimously.

His successor, C. Chesterfield, was a newcomer to the village, and had played with some success in 1936, as had his brother. Chris Turner remained as vice captain. When the question of the Lady Butler Cup arose, N.A. Chesterfield proposed that members should play in at least eight matches to qualify and that points should be allocated for performances at batting, bowling, fielding and wicketkeeping. The members with the highest number of points should then be entered into a ballot at the general meeting at the end of the season. When the committee met a week later Mr. Whalley-Tooker did attend and he pointed out that he had been captain for 43 (sic) years and he hoped that Chesterfield's term in office would be as long and would be successful! In reply the new skipper was proud to be captain of the oldest club in the world. The season was one of the most successful for many years, the final results showing 15 victories in 31 matches, as against eight losses. Chesterfield led from the front, scoring 405 runs at 25 per innings. He showed his best form in July, carrying his bat for 60 through the innings of 110 against a touring side Pembroke County, and followed this with an unbeaten 35 against Portsmouth United Banks, and he was always making useful scores. The same could be said of a number of the side, as there was a general improvement in the batting led as in so many previous seasons by Fred Hall. With so many bowlers available to attack the opposition there was less opportunity for outstanding bowling performances, but Turner continued to puzzle opponents, J. Smith returned a number of useful performances, while Hall, in a two innings game, followed an analysis of five for 33 with scores of 24 and 68 not out. F. Banting, H. Hooker and J. Treherne were also useful run makers. This season the club exceeded three figures in no fewer than 18 innings.

The most remarkable game was the one against Hambledon in Surrey who had been welcome opponents since 1934; the sides tied on 193 runs each, Fred Hall contributing another 50.

There was concern during the summer of 1937 about proposed alterations to The Bat and Ball. A committee meeting chaired by Mr. Whalley-Tooker on 26 April resolved that cricket lovers would feel it immensely to have the place modernised out of recognition, and detailed the secretary to write to Henty and Constable the brewery, and to Hampshire County Cricket Club and MCC. The responses from these bodies, as well as the views expressed by The Society For The Protection Of Ancient Buildings were judged by the committee to be quite satisfactory, and the brewery acted with great sensitivity, setting up a committee to monitor the alterations, which were complete by summer 1939.

On 5 July 1937 the club sent congratulations and best wishes to their President and Lady Butler who celebrated their diamond wedding on the 12th. The year ended with Mr. Whalley-Tooker suggesting to the general meeting that the club issue a challenge to the Australian tourists who were due in England in 1938 under the captaincy of Don Bradman. This did not come off, but the club were a little more successful when the West Indian cricketers visited in 1939.

In December 1937 Sir Thomas Butler died at the age of 90. He had been President since 1879 and had played for the club as long before as 1865, and on 11 March 1938 the general meeting stood in silence in tribute to his memory. His successor, hardly a matter for surprise was Mr. Whalley-Tooker. Among new vice presidents were Countess Peel, who, recently widowed, lived at Leydene House, so soon to be requisitioned and subsequently to form the heart of the land based naval establishment HMS Mercury, near East Meon; and the Revd A.C. Champion the new vicar of Hambledon who was an active cricketer and was soon induced to play for the club.

In the spring of 1938, the committee's first concern was the state of the wicket, resulting from, of all things, drought: as early as 20 April, the ground committee warned that the first match fixed for the 30th would have to be cancelled unless it rained by the 26th, and as there is no record of the fixture in the scorebook, cancelled it must have been. By the second week in May, water had to be carted to the ground, and the magnitude of the task led the club to ask Portsmouth Water Co. for permission for F. Bucksey the neighbouring farmer who was also a club member, to provide a supply of water.

Chesterfield showed continued good form with the bat, playing especially well for his 81 not out against Engineers Sports on 6 June, but by the end of the month his appearances were becoming spasmodic: nevertheless he played a major part in the installation of the mains water supply: on 10 August, at a poorly attended meeting of the committee he waded into the topic pointing out that the club was

Hambledon Cricket Club Team 1937. Back row standing: Rich Bucksey, A. May, 'Dabber' Hooker Jack Knight (Umpire), Jim Watson, George Wallace. Front row: Geoff Hartridge, Fred Banting, Chris Turner, Capt. Chesterfield (Capt.), Fred Hall, 'Punch' Smith, Mr. Hooker (Scorer).

fortunate in having skilled professional people in the side. George Wallace for example had first come to Hambledon in the early 1930s to install the village's electricity supply, he had stayed and was now an enthusiastic member of the committee. Fred Banting, a future captain of the club, was a plumber and the committee accepted his estimate of £24 for installation of a water tank, provided of course that Winchester College gave their consent: they approved the proposal for a rain water tank of 4000 gallons capacity with filter beds; the work was hurried on to completion and much hard labour spared. Would the club have ever done the job without the spur from Mr. Chesterfield?

The cricket in 1938 was again of good standard, 17 victories coming from 28 games, without a single draw. Defeats matched wins in the first eight matches, largely through frailty in batting and there were three defeats in succession in June, but there followed eight victories out of the next nine games with one loss followed by two more successes. The side had reached a high standard of all round work in which Fred Hall, Chris Turner, J. Smith and G. Hartridge excelled; Hall surpassed all his colleagues in consistency and when available, Chesterfield scored readily, as did the Revd Champion, but the strength of the team lay in the bowling as the averages show:

BATTING

	Inns	NO	Runs	High Score	Average
C. Chesterfield	10	3	205	81*	29.26
F. Hall	23	-	470	102	20.43
Revd A.C. Champion	17	3	241	71*	17.21
J. Smith	20	-	333	55	16.65
F. Banting	22	1	251	33	11.95
G. Hartridge	22	-	241	63	10.95
A. Hall	9	1	58	16	7.25
C. Turner	24	2	159	26*	7.22
S. Browning	12	3	65	15*	7.22
H. Hooker	13	1	68	24	5.66
G. Wallace	14	2	62	16*	5.16
B. Bucksey	9	2	32	19	4.57
J. Watson	15	1	58	25*	4.14

BOWLING

	Overs	Maidens	Runs	Wickets	Average
G. Hartridge	223	44	551	86	6.4
C. Turner	189.1	48	446	65	6.88
J. Smith	217.1	50	556	57	9.75
F. Hall	137.2	22	403	35	11.51

At the general meeting on 9 November 1938 there were six nominations for the Lady Butler Cup and in a ballot Fred Banting was elected. Hartridge won the Chesterfield fielding prize. Mr. Champion raised the question of installing a permanent practice wicket, and of arranging matches for 15-18 year olds. When the club reconvened in the spring, with Mr. Whalley-Tooker in the chair, Chesterfield resigned the captaincy as he was leaving the village and Mr. Champion was elected in his place. F. Beagley joined the committee and Lady Butler became a vice president. A sign of increasing prosperity was the decision that the team should be transported for the annual match at Hambledon Surrey by private car rather than coach. By this time both the other Hambledon, and Wadhams, still based at Broadhalfpenny Down were long term and popular opponents, and when the touring West Indians visited The Bat and Ball on 30 July and were entertained to tea, Wadhams were invited to send representatives. (The expenses of the occasion were as Mr. Whalley-Tooker put it, collected privately.) On the previous day Hambledon had beaten Wadhams by eight runs, the clubs total of 185 including scores of 39 by Banting, 38 by J. Watson, and 25 not out by A. Newland.

That weekends cricket represented the high point of a season, which came to an early end on 12 August. The club defeated Vospers in a match in which Smith took five wickets for 15 and Hew Butler hit up 26, and Southsea Wanderers (Smith six for 23), but lost by six wickets to the Nondescripts, Champion and Hugh Butler each scoring 26. The magnificent cricket played by A.V. (later Sir Vivian) Dunne, of Green Lane, cannot be overlooked for in five matches he scored 94, 17, 26, 20 and 90, acquiring in those five innings the seasons highest aggregate for the club, and followed his score of 26 against Southsea Wanderers with an analysis of eight wickets for 31.

The first class season continued for another two weeks, before its premature termination because of the declaration of War. It was a greatly diminished number of members (10) who attended a belated general meeting on 30 January 1940, under the chairmanship of the vicar. Severe winter weather kept Mr. Whalley-Tooker at home, so that he did not have the pleasure of hearing the report of another successful season in which 14 matches were won, eight lost and two drawn. Of the regular players, J. Smith headed the batting averages totalling 231 runs at an average of 17 with Mr. Champion a little behind him. A. Newland was the least expensive bowler, his 29 wickets each costing only 3.86. Chris Turner took his 63 victims at 9.34 runs each and he was awarded the Lady Butler Cup. There was a small balance on the right side financially even allowing for the £24 invested on the water tank. The grim times were lightened by a kindly action. The Chesterfield Fielding Cup was a contest between George Wallace and Billy Sayner, but the former, a generous spirit, withdrew in favour "of the young lad." He made another kind move in May, presenting the club with a new minute book. The full one dated back to 1907 and the days of J.A. Best, and the planning for the construction of the monument.

How much use would there be in 1940 for the new book?

Chapter 12
More War And A Recovery

In fact, 21 fixtures were arranged for 1940 thanks to Mr. Turner's efforts during the winter. In March though, he had to report that all but two had been cancelled, but the committee urged him to go back to the opposition, which he did with some success, to the extent that in the end eight games were played, of which the first four resulted in victory while the remainder were all lost. Hew Butler and Mr. Champion both scored runs, Chris Turner and Fred Hall turned in good all round performances, and G. Faithful was a new name to the forefront. There was a normal run of fixtures through to 6 June, followed by an undated game against the 22nd Regiment R.A.: there is then a break before one final match on 31 August 1940 against 36/55 Battery. The scores: the Battery 175, Hambledon 19. The names of that last Hambledon team deserve to be recorded. The team was R. Bucksey, A.C. Champion, W. Tanner, G. Faithful, C. Turner, F. Banting, A. Chambers, T. Green, J. Goldsmith, W. Sayner and J. Watson. It is as we shall see of some significance that the last two fixtures were against military teams.

The call-up, the retreat from Dunkirk at the end of May, intensifying troop movements, and enemy air attacks on Channel shipping soon ended any degree of normality in South Hampshire. There are no more recorded Hambledon matches until 1945, and no meetings between June 1940 and a general meeting on 21 April of the following year. On that occasion the eleven members who were present stood in silent tribute to their President Edward Whalley-Tooker, whose death at the age of 77 on 23 November 1940, Mr. Champion justly described as a tragic blow to the club. There was no aspect of its activity, or indeed of any major organisation in the village in which he had not been involved over nearly 50 years, while he had become a public personality through his participation in the big matches of 1908, 1925, 1929 and 1931 (to say nothing of his activities as a magistrate). The interval between his appearance for Hampshire in 1882, and the monument match of 1908 remains the longest between two successive appearances by a player in first class cricket. The meeting elected Mrs. Whalley-Tooker as his successor.

Mr. Champion also referred to an uncertain future. He told the meeting that it was most likely that troops stationed around Hambledon on route for overseas service, which would include personnel posted at Bury Lodge, the Butler family home, would use the ground: he suggested that they should be limited to one match a week and leave the ground in a proper manner and that management should be left to the club's ground committee. The idea had come from Mr. Turner the secretary whose intention it was to save the ground from being turned over to cultivation in the thrust to "dig for victory". The only other relevant event in the years of struggle as far as the cricket club was concerned was the visit of a drama group to the village in November 1944, the proceeds going to the benefit of the club on the initiative of Mr. Champion. Not only did he have tickets and posters printed at his own expense but he told the committee that provided that they helped with the arrangements, he would make up any loss. He did not have to: as the event was a great success raising around £12 (£240 in present day values) for the club, which enabled them to returf the square, put the mower in working order, and generally to be ready for better days to come when the war was at last over.

Mr. Champion did not wait for victory before taking the first steps to revive the club. As early as 21 February 1945 he called eleven club members to The New Inn and asked if they should make a start that season. Led by George Wallace and J. Watson, who became landlord of the The George Hotel, those present agreed to raise a side and formed a ground sub-committee composed of Watson, G. Faithful, Wallace, and Fred Banting, who also agreed to check and list the gear. A.J. May of the generation which had grown up during the war, said he would organise a whist drive (it raised £16) and that good friend of the club, Mr. Champion, directed the proceeds of the Easter Monday Fête to the club.

That February gathering fixed a general meeting for 21 March, when the attendance of 19 fulfilled all expectations. Major General Stephen Butler CB, CMG, DSO, who by then was living at Bury Lodge presided, E.J. Turner and A. Hall were re-elected as hon. secretary and treasurer, and Mrs. Whalley-Tooker continued as President. Mr. Champion did not stand again for the captaincy although he did go on to play some cricket that year and he proposed Fred Banting for the post, but in the democratic spirit of the times, Mr. Poole proposed Chris Turner. Any rivalry was dispelled when the nominees agreed that Turner should be vice captain.

Subscriptions were fixed at 3/6d (18 pence), 2/6d (12.5p) and 1/6d (7.5p) for full members, and those under 18 and 16 respectively. G. Hall resigned from the committee after 40 years of membership.

CHAPTER 12

The new committee faced a number of difficulties: at first fixtures were hard to come by, and mid May showed only six. Three adverts on successive nights in the Evening News, Portsmouth, were productive, as eventually the number increased to 18 matches, and by the time they started in early June, a matter of days after the allies sealed victory in Europe, only one Saturday was left blank.

There were more intimidating problems in those years of reconstruction. Almost everything was subject to regulations or rationing including milk, food, petrol, even cricket gear. In the spring J.E. Turner wrote to the Hampshire County Cricket Club, who were the nominated agency for the distribution of such cricket gear as was available, only to be told that all applications should have been received by the previous January! He had then to make an application to the Board of Trade but received no reply. He had also to write to the Food Office to ask if any rations could be made available to the club for tea. There was again no drinking water available at Brook Lane, and Mrs. Newland, who agreed to do the catering, had to carry out all the preparation at the Hall and have it taken to the ground by car. To add to the difficulties, the outfield was covered in rough grass after harrowing and the mower caused trouble over many months.

As spring moved into summer things gradually fell into place. The Board of Trade granted a license to purchase three bats and three balls, but rejected the application for gloves and pads, which certainly showed a correct order of priorities. Presumably the officials considered that the club was adequately provided for in protective equipment. The Food Office issued a permit for the purchase of milk, and the dairy's milk van served a dual purpose, as it also carried drinking water to the ground. Bill Sayner mowed the outfield, and the Royal Naval Station at Leydene loaned a motor mower and groundsman to tend the square.

That summer, two matters of discussion were the introduction of Sunday cricket, which met with little support, and the possibility of a return to Broadhalfpenny Down. The secretary wrote to Winchester College on that topic which was hotly argued at a rather sparsely attended committee meeting, before the members divided three/three, at which Richard Bucksey in the chair gave his casting vote against proceeding.

The season's results were unremarkable, the seven victories being outmatched by ten losses, but three of the defeats were by margins of less than 10 runs, and there was also one tie. The weakness in batting was even more noticeable than usual for, while G. Faithful averaged 23, he played only six innings and Ron Turner who came next and scored most runs, totalled only 155 at an average of 10. The bowling was a different proposition - four members of the attack took their wickets at an average of under 10 and those of Ron Turner who was as low as fifth in the table came out at only 12.25 each. He also held most catches and not surprisingly as the youngest member of the team in his first season, he was successful in the ballot for the Lady Butler Cup: the donor still alive in her 98th year may have marvelled at the passing of the generations.

During the winter the club received approaches from an old opponent and a new one. Downing College, Cambridge asked for a renewal of fixtures, a pleasant reminder of pre-war days and of Hyde Whalley-Tooker's participation of matches with his father. The Regency Cricket Club of Brighton sought an old time match with Hambledon during Brighton Carnival Week. In reporting this approach, J.E. Turner added that he had already accepted the challenge.

It is difficult to tell from the minutes what machinations or politics were involved in that years elections: Fred Banting was the captain in office but at the general meeting on 20 March 1946 he was faced with two opponents who both then withdrew leaving him in possession of the field. A.E. Hall who was re-elected as treasurer had been able to report a profit on the years working of nearly £41.

J.E. Turner complained about attendance at committee meetings over the previous year, which had been so low at times as to make it almost impossible to transact business: he even read out the individual attendances, which was embarrassing as the committee elections were yet to come. It was eventually agreed that the committee be increased from seven to nine, and that it should include two younger members of the club nominated by the committee, who should not have a vote and leave if a confidential matter arose. There was no embarrassment in the committee elections, as there were nine candidates for nine places. C. Bendall offered a bat for presentation to the best young all-rounder and the members favoured Faithful's suggestion that the opposing captain should nominate the best youngster after each match.

Mr. Turner must have been impressed at the size of the attendance, 14, at the next committee meeting, though even this was exceeded at some subsequent ones. He had obtained a certificate for new gear from the Ministry, and Messrs Hargreaves the outfitters from Portsmouth attended and in due course the committee selected two new bats at just under £3 each, another at less cost, two balls at just under £1.50 each and a set of stumps at the equivalent of 75 pence today but the value of money has diminished about 20 times since then.

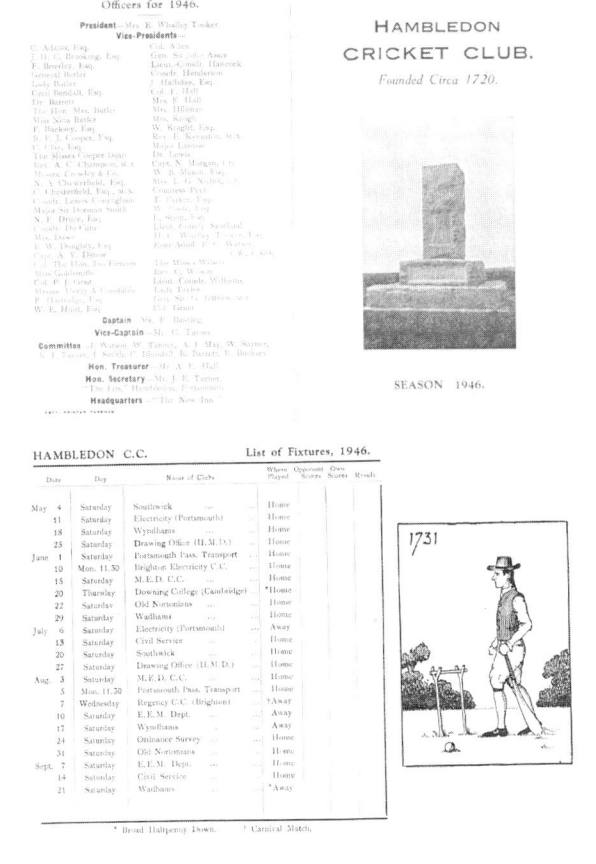

The Fixture Card for 1946

The summer was full of incident including the visit of a film company to record part of a match, preparation for the costume game at Brighton and a row over the clubs pictures and memorabilia, which were on display at The New Inn. The problem had come to light when Mr. Turner, accompanied by two reporters from the BBC (who were compiling a programme about the club, which was broadcast later in the year) asked the landlord, the inappropriately named Mr. Dry, for the return of an old print of Windmill Down. Mr. Turner had recovered the print in the face of opposition from the landlord, alarm bells rang in Mr. Turner's ears and he had asked Messrs Crowley the brewery, which pictures and prints were on the pubs inventory. They were not able to clarify the matter and Mr. Turner in his own words had an unsatisfactory interview with Mr. Dry, who claimed that the clubs items were included in the valuation when he took over the pub, and not surprisingly thought that they belonged to him. His offer to leave the treasures behind when he gave up the license was not very reassuring and the problem was not settled until February 1947 and then only by the brewery doing the decent thing and paying the landlord for the collection and designating it as the property of the club.

Then out of the blue, Wadham brothers offered to give way to the club if they wanted to use Broadhalfpenny Down and to swap grounds if Wadhams had a fixture of their own. The club elected Mr. Wadham a vice president, but their appearances on the Down did not noticeably increase.

As the festival at Brighton drew near, the players were measured for their period dress, transport was hired, and special practice was arranged for playing in XVIII Century mode. The match played on 12 August was a great success and was the first since 1931 to bring the club under the spotlight. It was a match of four-ball overs which were delivered underarm, played for an 18-gallon barrel of punch. Hambledon lost by 183 runs to 174.

As more decisions had to be made and committee meetings grew noticeably longer, J.E. Turner felt the strain and asked for an assistant. Astonishingly there was some opposition to this in committee, but he was authorised to nominate a member of the committee and he chose Cecil Blundell. In May 1946, the committee experienced an unusual problem - what the minute book describes as "an abundance of players." They considered selection by rota, but rejected it and when Dr. Lewis who was prominent in the club's counsels at the time proposed the appointment of a 2nd XI sub-committee, they turned that idea down as well, but A. May, one of the younger members, was authorised to arrange extra games in conjunction with the hon. secretary.

Amidst all this activity, which set the tone for the club's progress for years to come, the cricket was disappointing with only seven wins as against eleven defeats. The team could average only a little under 8 runs a wicket against opponents faring a little, but just sufficiently, better, at something under nine. H. Hooker a long standing member and then the regular scorer headed the batting averages playing in a few matches but Ron Turner with 189 runs, average 11 was the outstanding batsman and his average shows how hard the club found it to get runs. The pitch required constant treatment and did not favour batsmen, and the summer, one of the wettest on record, was also a contributory factor, so it was not surprising that the two leading bowlers, Chris Turner, and J. Smith, in his last season before leaving the village, returned such good figures:

	Overs	Maidens	Runs	Wickets	Average
Turner	177	48	359	43	8.35
Smith	208	64	402	46	8.83

The team which took the field for the first match of 1946 was Fred Hall, Chris Turner, S. Harding, G. Faithful, Ron Turner, J. Smith, J. Watson, W. Tanner, L. Stent, F. Banting and J. Gardner. Gardner began with a succession of startling bowling performances: four for nine against Southwick, who still won by 59 runs to 40, seven for nine against Portsmouth Electricity whose total of 21 Hambledon passed for the loss of one wicket, five for three which contributed to a similar victory over Wyndhams, six for 31 versus CDO, and five victims for six runs against Portsmouth Transport. The only notable batting total was the clubs 160 for nine declared in the drawn return game with Southwick and it was 3 August before one of the team achieved a score of 50, when Commander Evans hit up 51 not out against MEDCC. An outstanding performance came a week later when Hambledon set 78 to defeat EEM Hilsea, had sunk to 33 for seven: Richard Bucksey 23 not out and Gardner 48 not out made a winning stand and batted on to take the total into three figures.

That season resulted in a profit of £53, a good position in which to approach 1947, but a couple of quality batsmen were desperately needed. Chris Turner won the Butler Cup and Ron Turner the Cecil Blundell Bat for the best all-rounder under 21.

Fred Banting was re-elected as captain for 1947 after Messrs Tanner and Chris Turner withdrew, Tanner filling the role of vice captain. The issues of a 2nd XI and Sunday cricket were in the air, but this does not mean they got off the ground. In July the youthful Ron Turner told the committee that he had arranged three 2nd XI games and named his team: himself, A. Golding, K. Merrington, M. Taylor, R. Parvin, S. Parvin, A. Shawyer, R. Beagley, A. May, P. Parvin and R. Blackman. As for Sunday play, which was a proposition warmly supported by the Rev Champion, Dr. Lewis opposed it, but suggested that if any member wished to arrange a few Sunday games privately, that was another matter. The general meeting agreed to this fudge and as a result the scorebook contains several sheets marked "not to count in the averages." The doctor made a more positive proposal that the club build a permanent pavilion worthy of their status, and that they should open a pavilion fund offering the opportunity for donations and legacies, and investing any spare cash the club had. The suggestion was to bear fruit later.

The summer, which turned into a memorably hot one, began with what, a little later in drought conditions, could have been a major disaster, when, while the groundsman and several members were burning off rough grass from the outfield, the wind freshened and in spite of their efforts the fire spread into an adjoining field, burning off a large area. The secretary had to write an apology to Mr. Nichol, the tenant, and in May he had some more apologising to do following the cancellation of the first match of the season against Southwick, following what he described as the appalling weather during the few days preceding the match, which he called off at 7.30am on the day, which involved him in a cycle ride to Southwick to contact their secretary. A new mower had been ordered as the old one had given up the ghost and for weeks the club were without one due to delay on the part of the manufacturers. Preparation of the square became a real difficulty. J. Watson offered to fit another engine into the old mower, then when the suppliers still did not come up to scratch he went to a farm sale and bought a 30 inch mower for £30 unseen. He offered it to the club with some hesitation but it proved just what was wanted and the club had the pleasure of cancelling the manufacturers order. Mr. Blundell had helped raise over £100 by organising whist drives and a raffle during the winter, and the committee decided to invest the sum in the post office savings bank, to form the nucleus, not of a pavilion fund, but of a mower fund.

At the general meeting in November, J.E. Turner in his report described the playing record as not looking too good, the sides nine victories being quite outfaced by 14 reverses. There were still no drawn games but this is easily accounted for by the long hot summer and the weakness of the batting in a year when the highest batting average, that of H. Hooker, was 13 and the best aggregate, achieved by Ron Turner, only 256 runs. The death of Lady Butler at the age of 99 coincided with spirited competition for her award as there were six nominees: eventually two of them had a handful of equal votes, and Fred Banting in the chair had to appeal to all 17 members present to vote. H. Hooker was then elected by nine votes to six.

Chapter 13
Bowlers and Fund-Raisers

At the general meeting in February 1948, Fred Banting gave up the captaincy and was succeeded by W. Tanner with J. Watson as vice captain. The club's playing fortunes improved: administration also proved less demanding and committee meetings contained fewer pressing matters and they were often able to select teams for as many as five forthcoming fixtures at one monthly session. By July they felt confident enough to revive the annual cricket supper, which was fixed for November, the principle attraction being entertainment from the Pathfinder Concert Party. In the event the season's results, which showed an enormous improvement as victories 16, readily outweighed losses nine, justified the celebration. Another reason for satisfaction was the hon. secretary's return to duty, after some weeks' absence through illness, at the committee meeting on 15 November, when preparations were made for the general meeting and the supper which was to follow it. Admiral Bertram Chalmers Watson, CB DSO RN, who lived at the Court House in Hambledon, and was the father-in-law of Mr. Sykes who would become the club's landlord, chaired both events, presiding over 20 members at the meeting which heard that Philip May headed the batting, scoring 269 runs average 16, with Fred Banting second. The side's strength lay in the attack in a damp season when 80 was likely to be a winning total. The figures speak for themselves:

	Wickets	Average
K. Moon	24	4.79
W. Tanner	36	6.77
C. Turner	61	7.37
B. Barrett	56	8.35

But Philip May was awarded the Lady Butler Cup for the best batting form shown for the club since the war. Fred Hall was still a regular member of the side but did not score as prolifically as he had done before the war. His brother, Albert Hall, still the treasurer, reported a favourable balance of £160, thanks to zealous fundraising during the winter. The membership deliberated over two matters which engaged cricket administrators at that period; the first was the coaching of boys which was being promoted by MCC through the influence of Harry

Altham who was now on the committee of that club and was soon to hold the central post of treasurer, and was also President of Hampshire County Cricket Club. Hambledon resolved to have a concrete practice strip, which was in place by August 1948. The other topic was Sunday cricket which the general meeting agreed would be better run by the club, if it had to come, as it soon did. To start with, the club limited Sunday play to six fixtures.

As they moved into 1949 the secretary's health continued to cause concern and E. Lawrence was appointed his assistant. After missing a year Fred Banting was elected captain on the second ballot. The club received a challenge from Caterham Spartans Cricket Club in Surrey, whose secretary pointed out that fixtures between Caterham and Hambledon on their respective home grounds dated from 1767 and 1769. Hambledon picked up the gauntlet, and then issued a challenge of their own. As the oldest cricket club in existence they sent heartiest congratulations to Portsmouth AFC on winning the league division 1 championship and offered them an evening cricket match. The response is unrecorded.

Although the results do not always show it, the decade after the war was one of steady progress. The scorebooks for the period 1947 - 1961 are not available but from the fixture cards, team selections recorded in the minutes and his annual reports, we can tell that J.E. Turner worked steadily at improving the standard of the fixture list - and swiftly too. On two occasions when in the early autumn, Waterloo and Hedge End approached Hambledon with the prospect of a knock-out competition in 1949, Mr. Turner was able to tell the committee that the club already had a complete list for that season, and so there was no prospect of adding the knock-out to it (not that the club showed any enthusiasm for the project anyway). He was, on the other hand, always able to accommodate an offer which he thought good for the club, like the one from Caterham, and for the high profile period costume matches in which the club was asked to play during the fifties. Other features of the period include the almost continuous round of winter fundraising activities, whist drives, Christmas draws and dances, a special event being the New Year's Eve Dance, which was initially accompanied by records but later by the music of Mr. Gould, or the Hambledon Highland Band. A football lottery also proved a useful money-spinner. Prominent in the organisation of these funds was the ladies section headed by Mrs. Nolan and Miss.D. Hall. They had their own cricket practice nights, and fixtures, and both ladies were co-opted onto the committee. The New Inn remained the club's headquarters where the committee meetings were held. A feature of the club's constitution was that they had no formal office of chairman, whether for general meetings, of which there were still two a year, or for those of the committee. The chairman was selected on an ad hoc basis from those present, and this continued to be the case until 1961.

It was at the autumn general meeting that the election of the hon. secretary and treasurer, and nominations for the Lady Butler Cup took place, after the hon. secretary had given his summary of the season's play, including outstanding individual performances. The re-election of J.E. Turner and A. Hall was for 27 years from 1931 a forgone conclusion save for one notorious occasion after World War II when a rival candidate was unsuccessfully put up for the post of secretary. History does not record why this attempted revolution took place. As he continued to be unwell from time to time, his son R.J. (Ron) Turner, appointed assistant hon. secretary in 1951, increasingly attended meetings in his father's place.

The post war winners of the Lady Butler Cup were:

1945	R.J. Turner	1950	T. Tanner
1946	C. Turner	1951	R.J. Turner
1947	H. Hooker	1952	P. May
1948	P. May	1953	R. Ware
1949	P. Parvin	1954	K. Moon

As time went by the elections for the cup became more and more controversial and in the spring of 1955 the general meeting was informed that all the space for winners names on the trophy was used up. A short discussion about adding a band, or small shields to the plinth was brought to a sudden halt when a member suggested that the award had caused controversy at times and that increasing the space would be an expense. The truth was that members no longer felt enthusiastic about the annual award, and it was agreed that it be dropped and that the cup remain at headquarters. It was replaced by an award for club members under the age of 16 at the committee's discretion.

The interests of young players periodically came before the committee - usually when there was felt to be a dearth of them. An early reference was not very encouraging as at the autumn meeting in 1949, indeed, a club member suggested that a portion of the ground should be reserved for people who wished to watch the game in peace and quiet. He was assured that the committee would bear this in mind, and would definitely solve the problem before the next season, although how they intended to achieve this was not made clear. At the end of that year Bob Beagley, who was already closely involved in the running of the club, suggested that more 2nd XI games should be played, but the hon. treasurer told him that so few youngsters had paid subscriptions that it would be impossible to run a second string. When it was discovered that young non-members were using the club gear on Sundays, when, admittedly, few club matches were played, Bob offered to approach each individual and explain the position: no sub, no use of gear; but the problem was resolved only when 2nd XI fixtures were arranged for the season of 1950, using gear provided by Mr. Browning the village headmaster. After that, second team fixtures were arranged mostly in the evenings and in the summer holidays through the hard work of Jack Hall and R. Barrett.

2nd XI and ladies games contributed to increased wear on the pitch, which also suffered from time to time from the lack of a heavy roller and from an invasion, really an infestation, of moles, resulting in complaints from Mr. Nichol the neighbouring farmer, and in calling in the pest inspector: members of the club had to adopt an opportunist policy, keeping their eyes open for the presence of a road roller in the vicinity, as the driver could sometimes be persuaded to trundle up to Ridge Meadow and roll the square. On one occasion, the club hired a roller from Wickham but around lunchtime the Hambledon Bowling and Lawn Tennis Clubs highjacked the roller, resulting in frustration to the cricket club and argument as to responsibility for the bill which it required all the secretary's tact to resolve.

It was in the spring of 1955 that the committee really turned their minds to the condition of the ground and a period of intense activity followed. R. Ware chain-harrowed the outfield to spread the mole hills, and the committee gave a lead by turning up to clear stones, and to complete a brick store and lavatories as extensions to the pavilion. Yet all the time committee members had a niggling doubt about the club's security on the ground, for the need for maintenance and repair arose partly from the damage done by boys playing football there. The committee decided to raise the issue with the parish council and the Winchester College bursar in these words "How was our ground left, and what claim do we have to it?" The bursar replied direct to the clerk of the parish council (who had taken the precaution of raising a similar enquiry)

Winchester College
29 March 1955

Dear Sir,

<u>The Recreation Ground, Park, Hambledon</u>

I refer to your letter of the 24th March from which I am sorry to learn that a few irresponsible youths are causing concern by playing football over the cricket pitch.

I see the Broadhalfpenny Down Inclosure Award of 1857 imposes "the obligation of preserving the surface thereof in good condition and of permitting such land to be at all times used as a place for Exercise and Recreation for the Inhabitants of the said parish and neighbourhood".

After giving this matter careful consideration, I am of the opinion that the interests of "the Inhabitants of the said parish and neighbourhood" could be best maintained by their appointing a Committee to regulate the facilities afforded to them by the Award. I also feel that those living in the parish and the neighbourhood should decide upon the composition of such a Committee, i.e. whether this committee should be: -

(a) the members for the time being of the Hambledon Parish Council,

(b) representatives nominated by any existing (recreational) organisations, or

(c) a separately elected body.

A Committee as envisaged by (a) or (b) above would appear to have the advantage of permanency.

I can find no special reference to cricket in my copy of the Inclosure Award and, whilst I fully appreciate the concern of the Hambledon Cricket Club, I can think of no way in which the playing of cricket (and the appropriate preservation of the pitch) may be given preference over other recreations except by the formation of a Committee, as suggested, and that the Committee's "Regulations" should be confirmed by either the Parish Council(s) or the Rural District Council and be given the status of 'Bye-Laws'.

I note your suggestion that a small delegation might call to discuss the position with me, but I do not think any really useful purpose could be served by this because my considered opinion is that this matter is one which could be best dealt with locally on the basis I have suggested.

I presume the playing of football on the cricket pitch was the reason why the Assistant Honorary Secretary to the Hambledon Cricket Club wrote to me asking for my assistance, and I am therefore sending him a copy of this letter.

Yours Faithfully

(sgd) P. de LANDE LONG (Bursar)

The Clerk To The Parish Council

R.J. Turner the assistant hon. secretary reported that the parish council would be holding a general meeting with a view to framing byelaws for the ground, as the bursar had suggested. To the committee, this seemed like interference, but they could only await the outcome and in the meantime behaved with circumspection, raising no objection when Mr. G. Hartridge wanted to organise practice for the newly formed football club on the outfield (he had after all recently prepared a new practice wicket for club members). By October the parish council were awaiting advice from their legal advisor before looking into the possibility of seeking grant aid to purchase the ground. This was the time when the club's occupation of Brook Lane seemed most at risk because of the anxiety that the football club might have a call on the ground and pavilion during the 1955-56 season, but in May 1955 the council decided to take no further action.

The cricket club made some concessions to the footballers over the next two or three years, allowing them the use of ground and pavilion. However both cricketers and footballers had to turn their attention to fighting the moles, by the use of poisoned bacon, strychnine or traps or use the services of the pest control officer who deprecated all those methods, and yet did not himself come up with any effective suggestion. There were also problems with picnickers and steps were taken to keep out their cars by two bars placed across the entrance.

That the pitch was weighted in favour of bowlers is clear from the leading averages:

Batting
1949 F. Banting 399 runs, ave. 18.47
1950 P. May 252 runs, ave. 13.26
1951 R.J. Turner 338 runs, ave. 16.10
1952 R.J. Turner 574 runs, ave. 22.08
1953 G. Faithful 226 runs, ave. 28.23
1954 R.J. Turner 328 runs, ave. 14.91

Bowling
1949 W.G. Tanner 79 wickets, ave. 8.64
1950 B. Barrett 70 wickets, ave. 5.12
1951 T. Tanner 77 wickets, ave. 9.04
1952 T. Tanner 78 wickets, ave. 7.56
1953 R. Ware 68 wickets, ave. 10.44
1954 K. Moon 61 wickets, ave. 6.32

Except for 1949 all these seasons were wet above the average and accordingly helpful to the bowlers. Faithful played only eight completed innings in 1953, and Ron Turner's 1952 batting performance stands out like a beacon. Apart from him, no-one approached the figures achieved by Fred Hall in the 1930s. While no longer as prolific with the bat, Fred remained a useful member of the side.

Over the same period the overall results were:

Year	Played	Won	Lost	Drawn
1949	31	18	11	2
1950	34	15	17	2
1951	31	8	17	4
1952	33	17	14	2
1953	29	13	10	2*
1954	31	16	11	3*

*There was one tied match in 1954 and the figures for 1953 do not add up. Two matches were abandoned in 1951.

The club retained its appeal as an opponent for special occasions of which there were a number in the years after 1945. The first was the Brighton Festival challenge played in 1947. The second was more or less foisted on the club in Festival of Britain Year, 1951, when Admiral Watson asked HMS Mercury to provide the opposition for a match in old time style and costume. He appears to have contacted Hambledon after Mercury had agreed to play them and there was an initial lack of enthusiasm among the members for the idea. By April, when it formally came before the committee, Mr. Turner's fixture list was long complete and they gibbed at the information that management would be in the hands of an outside committee. Eventually Mr. Turner found a niche in his fixture list on 16 June and the club were represented on the committee. The team selected was W.G. Tanner (captain), Fred Hall, Major Knight, Ron Turner, Philip May, T. Tanner, Brian Bucksey, K. Moon, R. Barrett, Chris Turner and P. Parvin with H. Hooker as volunteer 12th man. A. Edney was the umpire, Mavis May conventional scorer, and Jack Hall scored by notching a stick, just as Stumps Turner had done for the HMS Nelson match in 1931.

A week later there was some dismay when a prominent member of the club expressed his surprise, and rather more, at his non-selection, and resigned from the committee, "subject to an explanation". Eventually he was pacified by an offer by a team member to stand down in his favour. The Admiral, who had to sit through this at a committee meeting, was then able to give his report on the final arrangements.

The match was a great success raising £150 for naval charities, and although the club's finances did not benefit, the Admiral did not forget them two years later in Coronation year. The first reference to another old time match came in December 1952. This time the clouds of pessimism soon lifted and the game, against the Combined Insurance Companies of London, subsequently renamed more romantically as the Ancient Firemen (after the crew who would come and put your fire out but only if you had their sponsors insurance), took place on Broadhalfpenny Down on 30 May. This time club funds, as well as naval and insurance charities, were to benefit. The Hambledon XI, selected well in advance, to enable a handsome souvenir programme to be printed - and period clothing to be fitted - was R.J. Turner, F. Hall, P. Parvin, P. May, K. Moon, B. Brown, G. Hartridge, B. Barrett, W. Tanner, R. Barrett and R. Beagley, the last two being selected by ballot.

An honoured invitee to these occasions was the 87-year-old R.P. Nyren, a retired bank manager, and the great-grandson of John Nyren and on one occasion at least he was asked to bowl the first ball of the match, but on account of age he felt unable to accept.

Hambledon were careful to practice for these old time events, using specially made curved bats and getting the feel of the garb. Coronation year was not famous for its fine weather, and the play was interrupted, but again a very large crowd turned up on Broadhalfpenny Down to see Hambledon enjoy the best of a draw. They scored 208 for seven declared, Ken Moon 96, which was a great feat for the left hander wearing unaccustomed costume and using the old style bat. The Ancient Firemen gave him no quarter, although he was so near the century and they replied with 167 for eight and after the game they entertained their hosts to dinner at The New Inn. In July Admiral Watson handed over a cheque for £33, the club's share of the profits.

That summer the club also took part in a pageant of sport on Southsea Common for which they again donned old style costumes and they dressed up once more for a match at the end of July in response to a challenge from Islip, the Oxfordshire club.

As a result of the Ancient Firemen's match and the hard work put in during the previous winter, Mr. Hall still the hon. treasurer, was able to point to a profit on the year's work of £145, with income exactly

CHAPTER 13

TEAMS

The Men of Hambledon	The Ancient Firemen (Cuaco Club)
R. J. TURNER (Capt.)	H. J. PLUCK (Capt.)
F. HALL	B. GRAINGER
P. PARVIN	G. H. LUMLEY
P. MAY	G. GOBEY
K. MOON	M. J. ALLIGHAN
B. BROWN	R. E. WALLER
G. HARTRIDGE	A. G. CRANCH
W. TANNER	J. R. PORTER
R. BARRETT	W. C. HULL
B. BARRETT	G. F. SMITH
R. BEAGLEY	D. W. SMITH

Umpire:
    F. BROWN

Notcher:
    C. TURNER

Umpire:
    J. R. BISSETT

Notcher:
    N. S. SALTER

Refreshments will be obtainable on the ground

Luncheon Interval - 1.15 p.m.—2 p.m.   Tea Interval - 4.30 p.m.—5 p.m.

Programme – the team: Hambledon v. the Ancient Firemen, 30 May 1953, on Broadhalfpenny Down.

– 113 –

doubling outgoings; indeed over these years the club's finances prospered in line with its growing reputation on the field. Usually the club won at least as many matches as they lost with the notable exception of 1957 when the club had only six victories against 15 defeats. The reasons for this were not hard to find as the highest batting average, achieved by R. Ware, was only a little over 16 and the average runs per wicket amounted to as little as 8.4, whereas opponents managed 11.30, or nearly 30 runs an innings more than Hambledon and, worse still, this was one of the few seasons when bowlers were not able to make up for the deficiencies of the batsmen. It is interesting to contrast that season with the following one, one of the wettest summers on record, when their average runs per wicket were almost exactly the same as in the previous year, but the attack was more than equal to the situation, confining the opposition to an average of 6.5. The bowlers responsible were:

	Overs	Maidens	Runs	Wickets	Average
Robert (Topsy) Turner	305.5	97	568	107	5.31
Bernard Brown	318.3	101	524	87	6.02

In 1957, Albert Hall expressed a wish to resign the treasurership which he had held for so long. He was pressed to continue for one more year, completing the span of 32 seasons, but at the general meeting in October 1958 he nominated Ken Moon, an architectural technician, as his successor. The club acknowledged Mr. Hall's services by electing him an honorary life vice president of the club.

The club mourned an even greater loss in February 1960 with the death of J.E. Turner. He had been in failing health for some years and was seldom seen at committee meetings, but carried out correspondence, made fixtures, and wrote up the minutes at home, at The Firs, in accordance with information received from his son, Ron Turner, who attended the meetings as assistant secretary. Turner senior had acted as hon. secretary for as long as 29 years, spanning the 2nd World War, and several generations of cricketers, and had worked assiduously on behalf of the club since he inherited a non existent fixture list in the spring of 1931. His loss might have left an aching void but Ron Turner, who already had so much experience of the club's affairs, was fortunately available to be elected in his place.

For the whole of the club's recorded history up to 1955, the full committee met fortnightly. Among their duties was the selection of teams for future fixtures, sometimes dealing with as many as six in one meeting. The system worked well, and there are few references to shortages of players, or cancellation of matches, but the process must have taken the full committee a good deal of time and in June 1955 D.V. Weekes, a committee member, proposed that a selection committee should be set up "to remove this sometimes lengthy item from the general committee agenda." This proved controversial and an amendment by Bob Beagley that "such a selection committee, in addition to the general committee, be selected at a general meeting, but this seasons team selection continue as at present" was carried and effectively shelved the idea. The burden on the general committee was lightened when they decided to cancel their evening matches, in view of the difficulty in raising an evening team, which reads a little oddly in view of the club's future competition successes. One unusual custom still continued: the election of the chairman took place on an ad hoc basis at the start of each meeting, whether it was a committee or general meeting. For a long period up to the early 1960s Jack Hall, who had retired from long service in the Royal Navy and was employed at HMS Mercury, almost invariably took the chair, although Mr. Weekes and G. Hartridge stood in, particularly on occasions when both Turners were away, and Hall acted as secretary.

While midsummer trips to Caterham continued to attract publicity, the most widely known matches of the late fifties were those against Dartford, Kent, played at Hesketh Park, Dartford, on 9 September 1956 with the return played on Broadhalfpenny Down on 14 July 1957 and organised primarily for the benefit of Leo Harrison the Hampshire wicket-keeper. Admiral Watson again undertook the initial spade work, Ron Turner, Ray Barrett and Bob Beagley were deputed to join a committee and in May the club nominated five members who were to play in combination with Roy Marshall, Colin Ingleby-Mackenzie, Desmond Eagar, Vic Cannings and Jim Bailey plus the Winchester College batsman Rex Chester. Ron Turner, Fred Hall, R. Ware, Bernard Brown and G. Ridgewell were selected. Other club members acted as programme sellers and car park attendants. There was no reference to gate men - not at that stage anyway. Yet again an enormous crowd flocked to the Down and the game, favoured with reasonable weather, looked to be a financial success, but after the event the agreed division of the profits caused the committee some anxiety, for while Leo's share amounted to £75, and naval charities were to receive £25, it looked as if meagre pickings indeed would be left for the club out of the net profit

Grand Bi-Centenary Cricket Match
(1757 — 1957)

on Broad Halfpenny Down
Sunday, 14th July, 1957.

HAMBLEDON v. DARTFORD

Programme: Hambledon v. Dartford 1957.

of £104, especially as there was a possibility that the cost of advertising would wipe out the balance. Eventually adjustments were made and the club came out on the right side with a small balance of £8. However they did not feel equal to taking part in a similar game in 1958.

Hambledon had been without trophies since competition for the Lady Butler Cup had been given up, but when at the spring general meeting in 1958, Mrs. Wilson offered one cup, the members agreed to buy another, one to be for the best batting average achieved by a member playing a minimum of 15 innings and the other for the lowest

HAMBLEDON CRICKET CLUB
Founded Circa 1720
Affiliated to Hants County C.C.

Committee—Messrs. J. Hall, D. Taylor, L. Lilley, R. Barrett, B. Barrett, J. Banting.
Hon. Treasurer—Mr. K. C. Moon.
Gear Manager—Mr. R. Beagley.
Hon. Secretary—Mr. R. J. Turner, The Firs, Hambledon, Portsmouth.
Headquarters—'The New Inn'. Tel. 466.

SEASON 1960

FIXTURES 1960

Date	Day	Opponents	Gd.
April 24	Sun.	Waterlooville	A
30	Sat.	Portsmouth Bohemians	H
May 1	Sun.	Compton	H
7	Sat.	Portsmouth Banks	H
14	Sat.	Widley and Purbrook	A
15	Sun.	Curdridge	A
21	Sat.	H.M.S. Mercury	*A
22	Sun.	Caterham	A
28	Sat.	H.M.S. Dryad	A
29	Sun.	Hedge End	H
June 4	Sat.	Waterlooville 2nd XI	H
6	Mon.	Downside Wanderers	H
11	Sat.	Old Portmuthians	H
12	Sun.	Droxford	A
18	Sat.	Waterlooville 2nd XI	A
19	Sun.	West Ashling	H
25	Sat.	H.M.S. Mercury	H
26	Sun.	H.M.S. Dryad	H
July 2	Sat.	Yorkshire Nomads	H
3	Sun.	Denmead	A
9	Sat.	Widley and Purbrook	H
10	Sun.	Wiltshire Moonrakers	H
16	Sat.	Emsworth	H
17	Sun.	Alverstoke	H
19	Tues. 6 p.m.	Grammar School Masters	H
23	Sat.	Knowle	A
24	Sun.	Curdridge	H
30	Sat.	Wickham	H

FIXTURES 1960—continued

Date	Day	Opponents	Gd.
Aug. 1	Mon.	Havant Rovers	H
6	Sat.	Alverstoke	A
7	Sun.	Emsworth	A
13	Sat.	Old Portmuthians	A
14	Sun.	Droxford	H
21	Sun.	Portsmouth Press Club	H
27	Sat.	Denmead	H
28	Sun.	Compton	A
Sept. 3	Sat.	D. Gould's XI	H
4	Sun.	Portsmouth Bohemians	A
11	Sun.	South Hants Touring Club	H

Saturday, 24th June, 1967, v. Caterham at Caterham.
Bicentenary of Match played at
Caterham Common (1767).

Saturday, 21st June, 1969, v Caterham at Hambledon.
Bicentenary of Match played at
Hambledon (1769).

*Broadhalfpenny Down.

All matches 2.30 p.m. start unless stated.

Captain   Vice-Captain
Mr. R. Beagley   Mr. K. Moon
Umpire—Mr. T. Bulpitt
Scorer—Graham Barrett

Fixture list 1960 season. See the note "Founded circa 1720"

average attained by a bowler in at least 75 overs. The batting trophy was awarded to Robert Turner at the end of that season (and we have already seen that Topsy took over 100 wickets in 1958) but a bowling cup was not yet available. A member, R. Baker, offered a cup for award to Fred Hall, who captained the side in 1958 and 1962, in recognition of the number of times he had won the Lady Butler Cup as the best all-rounder. In the following year his renewed good form enabled him to win the batting trophy, which was a remarkable achievement for him, after nearly 40 years' service with the club.

Fred Hall's career with the club went back to the days of horse drawn transport when each spring the secretary obtained tenders for the hire of transport to away matches, but in 1959 coach transport was abandoned as sufficient cars were available.

The arrangements for the previous water supply had lapsed and in 1957 Bill Sayner was prevailed upon to bring water to the ground. Not until 1960 was an approach made to Mr. Sykes, the new tenant of Park Farm, to reconnect the supply. During the 1950s Hambledon made a number of approaches to the College about a return to Broadhalfpenny Down, heartened by the fact that Wadhams who had played there for 20 years, gave up in 1954. However to the disappointment of the club HMS Mercury became tenants: by 1960 they had their own ground at Leydene and, encouraged by this, the club again asked the bursar if they could return to their historic place of origin, only to be told that it was unlikely that Mercury would give the ground up. Yet there were always good reasons for remaining settled at Brook Lane where the club had, after all, had their base for over 100 years, and the pitch and facilities were gradually improved. For example a number of Hambledon enthusiasts formed a committee to work for the erection of what was described as a recreation hut in the village and they urged the cricket club to liaise with the village hall committee to raise money for the construction of a new outdoor practice strip at the ground. The result of this co-operation was that the ground was enhanced when this strip was laid down and available for practice in April 1960.

Chapter 14
Desmond Eagar - President

In March 1962 Mrs. Dorothy Whalley-Tooker died after over 20 years as President, and the committee invited E.D.R. Eagar to succeed her. His acceptance was a great coup for the club, and for 15 years he presided over their fortunes, literally at their annual general meetings but also as an overseer, and a very active one at that, of many aspects of the life of the club, publicising it whenever he could and stimulating activity particularly in fundraising. Desmond Eagar was well placed to help Hambledon: something of a cricket prodigy, he progressed from the Cheltenham XI to an Oxford Blue in 1939, and played for Gloucestershire under the captaincy of Walter Hammond. After the war he was the choice of the Hampshire committee to take over as captain of the County Cricket Club and he led the side from modest beginnings in 1946, to the highest position they had ever achieved - 3rd in the County Championship in 1955. He continued as secretary of the County Club after his retirement from the captaincy and his associations with cricket and cricketers spread well beyond the boundaries of Hampshire. He was a man of enthusiasm and energy who left no stone unturned to promote the interests of both the County and Hambledon, and, incidentally, he first led the club into looking beyond the immediate area for young players, encouraging the club to seek young men from Portsmouth Grammar School.

Once he became the club's presiding genius, things as Bob Beagley put it started to change. Within a month of his nomination he attended his first committee meeting and the secretary recorded "acquainted himself with the club in all respects with numerous questions some answered and some remaining to be answered, and outlined future possibilities to regain some status."

The list of vice presidents came under his scrutiny and the names of those who did not subscribe were pruned, and John Arlott, Harry Altham and the former County captain W.G. Lowndes were added. Eagar inspired the club to approach Mr. Bucksey about running a water supply to the ground and to contact the water company about the cost. Mr. Bucksey was prepared to allow the pipe laying but would not grant Formal Legal consent for it, which meant that the club might spend £250 or £300 on the installation and yet have no legal right to maintain their water supply. The pavilion, by this time something of an antique, and endearingly described by Eagar as a cow shed, was no longer adequate for an increasingly prosperous and well-known club. The initial idea for a replacement, the purchase of a hut from Plessey, was soon dropped in favour of a brick building and by January 1964 Eagar had introduced the committee to the idea of an application to the National Playing Fields Association for grant aid towards installing the water supply as well as rebuilding the pavilion. The club set up a development committee consisting of Len Lilley, K. Moon, Bernard Brown and Ron Turner and they made a submission to John Pell of the Hampshire Playing Fields, which he referred on for a grant. One issue which was bound to raise its head at this stage was the club's lack of secure tenure at the ground. The President was again to the fore suggesting that they offer non-playing or life membership to a wide range of enthusiasts in return for a donation of £10 and that the club have its own tie for presentation to subscribers, together with a personal letter of welcome from him. As will be seen, donations and sales raised significant sums in short time and were of great advantage to the club's finances in the long term.

The club's profile remained high. In 1961 Southern Television prepared a short feature on the club showing the members going about their normal day-to-day activities, and shots of the village and of some of the games. The BBC did something similar a few years later but the best remembered function is one which owed a great deal to a formidable combination of Desmond Eagar, John Nyren and Harry Altham. The year 1964 was the bi-centenary of the birth of Nyren the chronicler of the XVIII Century Hambledon club and the committee decided to commemorate the anniversary with a dinner at the village hall. Desmond Eagar asked Harry Altham to be the principal speaker and invited R.E.S. Wyatt, the former captain of Warwickshire, Worcestershire and England, and Colin Ingleby-Mackenzie, leader of the Hampshire side which had won the Championship in 1961.

The occasion gave Harry Altham the opportunity to display his pre-eminence as cricket's foremost historian, as well as his wit and his love of the game. Of John Nyren he said "His pen has brought to life the great men whose achievements still dominate the history of our national game" and he ended with this tribute "He conjures for us the May days of cricket and his words are just as vivid today as when he wrote them."

Hambledon around 1959. Front row: F. Ware, Ray Barrett, Bob Beagley, Dave Taylor, R. Ware, Graham Barrett. Back row: Umpire, B. Brown, John Banting, ?, Colin Barrett, Henry Clarke and Ron Turner.

A hard act to follow, but Bob Wyatt managed it, discussing the progress - or otherwise as he rather implies - of cricket since his own playing days had begun in the 1920s. Colin Ingleby-Mackenzie's speech took on a serious note when he said "The mental approach is what determines a game, and I am afraid it seems to be a negative one at present". So ended a memorable occasion.

From this time onwards winter entertainments became more numerous, consisting of dinner dances, organised to show appreciation of the work done by the ladies during the season, but in the seventies, these functions gave way to discos, which were usually held at the Curzon Rooms, Waterlooville and in later years at Clarence Pier, Southsea.

Meanwhile in the committee room the haul was to be a long one. The committee became nervous at the proposals of the football club to use the ground even thought they were, it was discovered, limited to pre-season practice. This was a further reminder that the club's hold on Brook Lane was precarious and as the committee noted in the autumn of 1964, "improvements to our ground will be pointless unless we have control of it." This was emphasised when the Department of Education and Science notified the club that a grant for a new pavilion would most

Hambledon CC, winners of the Petersfield Knock Out Cup, 1968.
Back row; David Taylor, John Lloyd, John James, Bob Beagley, Bernard Brown, Len Marchant, Bob Munton, Dave Dunham.
Front row: Colin Barrett, John Banting, Ron Turner, Robert Turner.

likely be made available if "Winchester College would give them a lease of the present ground." It was Desmond Eagar who volunteered to take up the matter with the College and with Harry Altham. The College bursar's reply was not encouraging. It was unlikely that any lease of Park Farm could be offered to enable any grant to be obtained, and he raised what turned out to be a red herring which diverted the club from its main purpose - the improvement of Brook Lane - with the suggestion that efforts might be directed to a return to Broadhalfpenny Down.

The committee heard this notion with enthusiasm, yet HMS Mercury had been firmly in place as tenants there for 12 years, there was no suggestion that they intended to give it up, or that the College were prepared to oust them, and they were to remain there for many years. So by the spring of 1966, the total improbability of obtaining more than just a few odd games a year on the historic down (which is what Mercury were to suggest), coupled with the necessity of improving the water supply to Ridge Meadow where water was still being carried in five gallon containers, led the committee to plump once and for all for continuation of play there.

It was then that a long and determined campaign for improvement to the facilities began in earnest. The provision of the piped water supply was the first objective and Desmond Eagar drafted a letter to The Cricketer magazine and Playfair Cricket Monthly appealing for more non playing members to help with fundraising. He sent a carefully worded application for funds to the Lords Taveners before setting out a further appeal to the 150 life and non playing members to renew their subscriptions: when the water supply was connected in June, the cost of £202 had been covered by donations.

A building committee made up of P. Rider, D. Taylor, K. Moon and Ron Turner began preparing for the construction of the new pavilion with the aid of a further grant from Hampshire Playing Fields. Other fundraising included a proposed door-to-door collection in Hambledon itself (which had to be abandoned because it was against the law) and an approach to local notables for loans or guarantees, which received a generous response, and a round of dances and jumble sales and the Christmas draw were all effective fundraisers. Eagar had still not finished: as a result of his further efforts the club received a donation of 100 guineas (£105) from Warwickshire Supporters Association while Leicestershire Cricket Society sent £25 as the result of a speech he made to them.

Hambledon 1969. Back row (left to right): M. Gaffney, A. Freud, E. Chaplin, P. Tompkins, D. Taylor, C. Lutyens, B. Barrett (scorer). Front row: T. Apperley, W. Ware, R. Beagley (captain), R. Turner, A. Maclean.

The funds stood at £1000. Fred Banting's estimate for a basic cedar building, with club members doing as much of the work as lay within their skills, was £900 but in addition preparation of the base and drainage would cost £890. P. Parvin was asked to supervise the work. A further problem had to be overcome when after the granting of planning permission for a new pavilion on the site of the old, both the College as owners, and Mr. Sykes the tenant, insisted that the new site should be "in the actual field" as Mr. Sykes put it, reminding the club that the original had been built in 1881 in a small enclave which never formed part of the land included in the inclosure award.

By January 1969 construction was sufficiently far advanced for a date to be fixed for a formal opening ceremony on Sunday 22 June when Ronald Aird MC was invited to perform it. He was for many years a prominent figure in cricket first as a good bat for Eton, Cambridge and Hampshire and then in succession assistant secretary, secretary and finally President of MCC. He also became President of Hampshire. Hambledon's opponents on the day were Caterham who had first played against Hambledon in 1767 (the actual bi-centenary

The formal opening of the Pavilion, 22 June 1969. On veranda: Jack Hall (left), Ronald Aird and Desmond Eagar. Seated, in white coat, Mrs Hall. Standing, in light jacket, John Pell, Hon Secretary Hampshire Playing Fields Association.

*The Hambledon and Caterham team at their Bi-centenary match, 22 June 1969. Front row (left to right): A. Westall(C), D. Taylor (H), G. Astle (C), R. Turner (H), E. Chaplin (H), M. Baloo (C), H. May (H), L. Hutchings (Chairman of Caterham C.C.). Middle row: P. Edwards (scorer, C), J. Banting (Umpire, H), G. Charman (C), R. Chadd (C), B. Firth (C), M. Gates (C), P. Tomkins (H), R. Ware (H), J. James (H), N. Bessey (umpire, C), B. Barrett (scorer, H), K. Moon (treasurer, H). Back row: M. Barks (C), A. Jessup (C), P. Jones (C), D. Astle (C), R. Turner (H), C. Barrett (H), D. Dunham (H), L. Marchant (H).
Key: (C) - Caterham, (H) - Hambledon.*

game was abandoned following torrential rain). On this occasion there was to be no old time costume. The pavilion was complete by May, J. Banting built a new scoreboard and presented it to the club and on Desmond Eagar's suggestion Bob Beagley purchased a flag to fly from the new flagpole. The Hambledon team was selected by ballot. Initially ten names emerged: Ron Turner, Robert (Topsy) Turner, W. Ware, Dave Dunham, D. Taylor, J. James, Colin Barrett, R. Munton, L. Marchant and H. May. The eleventh place was kept open until the committee had assessed the performance in the field of E. Chaplin, a new member. He satisfied the critics and was given the eleventh place while in the event P. Tomkins replaced R. Munton.

On a fine sunny day after lunch at The Bat and Ball and in front of a crowd of five or six hundred spectators, Caterham were successful by six wickets. At teatime Ronald Aird declared the pavilion open and was presented by Jack Hall with two bottles of wine from Sir Guy Salisbury-Jones's Mill Down vineyard. The College bursar and Mr. Sykes were honoured guests, and the visitors were entertained to supper at The New Inn, for so long the club's headquarters, where, according to one informant "a table which appeared to stretch almost the length of a cricket pitch groaned under the fare provided". This highly successful event resulted in a profit of £45 which when added to the existing fund meant that £400 could be paid straight away to reduce the sum of £620 outstanding in respect of the building costs.

That year 1969 saw another memorable dinner held on 25 November when the speakers were John Woodcock of Longparish, the distinguished cricket correspondent of The Times, the Hampshire captain Roy Marshall, Commander John Goldsmith, Hambledon's historian, who is the son of Commander Goldsmith of HMS Nelson, 1931 fame, and Desmond Eagar. Sir Guy Salisbury-Jones, who had held an open day in the vineyard for the pavilion fund donated 18 bottles of Hambledon wine, white, dry and slightly effervescent for consumption by the 66 diners.

Thirty years later the pavilion, greatly extended, is still an adornment to the ground, and a memorial to the imagination and effort of those visionaries of the 1960s, among them Desmond Eagar.

Chapter 15
Open To Competition

At the annual general meeting in March 1970 Ron Turner, after describing the previous twelve months activity as probably the greatest year for interest and achievement since the early days of the club's history, paid tribute to Desmond Eagar: his personal effort and enthusiastic support had made it all possible and the club owed him a great debt which must not be forgotten: sentiments received with acclamation by the members.

The 1960s had been years of improvement both in the strength of the fixture list and (as a result) in the standard of play. Previously victories usually balanced defeats, but in 1962 17 successes well outnumbered the 11 defeats, while in 1964, described by Ron Turner as the most successful season for many years, eight defeats were completely put in the shade by as many as 25 triumphs. Only one match was drawn. This was the result of consistent all round work, in which Robert (Topsy) Turner excelled. He was second in the batting to his namesake Ron Turner and also headed the list of wicket takers with 74 victims. He, Bernard Brown and H. Clark all captured their victims at under eight runs apiece. The following year was again successful, for victories, at 17, more than doubled losses. It is now clear that Topsy Turner had the most successful batting figures ever for the club up to that time, accumulating 753 at an average of 39, figures which not even Fred Hall in the 1930s had approached. He was also the leading wicket taker securing 70 victims at 8.3, only Len Marchant with 57 wickets at 6.4 coming above him.

Ron Turner continued his search for more challenging opposition, which probably accounts for the decline in 1966 and the poor season in the following year when only eight victories were recorded. However Colin Barrett scored 649 runs at 34 an innings, and Topsy Turner with 703 runs was not far behind. The team would have been stronger if Harry May and Len Marchant who together formed a penetrating opening attack had been regularly available. The side had returned to full excellence by 1970 when victories exceeded defeats by 20 to 14.

The batting in that season showed:

> Robert Turner with 667 runs, average 35
> Dave Dunham with 331 runs, average 16
> Ron Turner with 235 runs, average 15
> Colin Barrett with 440 runs, average 15

and the bowling:

> Robert Turner with 69 wickets, average 10
> R. Munton with 34 wickets, average 11
> L. Marchant with 42 wickets, average 11
> J. James with 42 wickets, average 13

The average runs per wicket attained by the club were at 13.44 a little better than those of opponents.

The period was one of increasingly competitive cricket. The first indication of this was the club's organisation of a single wicket competition in 1964. 16 club members competed; in the semi-finals, Colin Barrett (47) beat Bernard Brown (6) and Len Marchant (11) overcame Topsy Turner (1) before winning the competition with 35 to Colin Barrett's 14. The finalists were presented with tankards donated by Mr. T. Bulpitt, the club umpire. The event was repeated in several subsequent seasons. In the spring of 1967 the club joined the newly fledged Petersfield District Association of Umpires, which instituted a knockout competition in which Hambledon became enthusiastically involved. In the following year they reached the final in which, on 29 July, they defeated Greyshott by 83 runs to 64, and the trophy was proudly displayed in Mrs. Muntons drapers shop window. This success led to a challenge from the winners of the Medstead Knock-out, Hyde Ramblers of Winchester. Hambledon picked up the gauntlet and the match was played on 5 August when they were more than equal to the task, winning by six wickets in the last of the 16 eight ball overs. In 1968 they again progressed well through the Petersfield Knock-out playing five rounds before being eliminated.

In 1972 the club applied to participate in the newly formed Cricketer Haig National Village Championship, but that is for a later chapter. All this activity meant increasing demands on committee members and fundraisers (in some instances the same individuals).

Fundraising events out of season recurred with regularity: an autumn jumble sale, a dance, and a Christmas draw always proved successful, even if the organisers sometimes complained of lack of support from the cricketers themselves. To demonstrate some figures, in 1962 the jumble sale realised over £22, the draw brought in £31 and raised the club's credit balance to over £96, which increased to £164 a year later and £276 by the end of 1964. By 1966, when the improvements to the ground were in the offing the careful husbandry of Ken Moon had seen a years profit of £370 with cash in the bank of £724, and the coffers were then well topped up by profits on the jumble sale of £61 and the draw of £57 in 1968. In March 1970 the hon. treasurer was able to show £374 in hand, after paying all the expenditure on the pavilion.

The saying that coming events cast their shadows before was exemplified in July 1967 when the County Cricket Club invited clubs in the Portsmouth area to attend a meeting which was to "investigate and report to the County Club's general committee on ways in which the County Club can take the lead in raising the standard of club cricket and strengthen the liaison generally between the County Club and club cricketers in the County." The initial effort was a failure as out of the 28 clubs invited, only Hambledon and Denmead were represented but Desmond Eagar wearing his Hampshire hat did not give up. In April 1971 the club received details of a proposal to start a Hampshire league for Saturday play beginning in 1973. This time it was Hambledon's turn to hang back: they decided to be represented at the preliminary meeting and to express interest, but without committing themselves "until more is known of likely clubs and grounds." So their initial reaction was simply to confirm that they would possibly be interested; but after Ron Turner with Bob Beagley attended the inaugural meeting of the league, the club committee decided to make a formal application for entry. They did not apply to be placed in the regional league but when they found that that was where they had finished up, without any prior consultation, the club went into full retreat and decided to limit themselves to friendlies. The committee's view was clearly expressed in the minutes: "with good facilities we had little to lose in waiting to see the effect of the league" and that is what they did, when the Hampshire Cricket Association League started in 1973.

The committee were still looking to strengthen their hold on the ground. In September 1972 their application to register Ridge Meadow as common land was granted by the County Council, following the withdrawal of two formal objections, one a frivolous intervention by a person in Gosport, and the other on strict legal grounds from the council itself, who pointed out that the public footpath running inside the south eastern boundary must be excluded and the club had to agree. The registration resulted from a piece of invaluable advice given by an official in the Department of Education and Science which marked the beginning of the club's successful attempt to become owners of the ground.

Meanwhile the amount of play went on increasing so that complications arose from congestion of fixtures. They had a pretty lengthy fixture list already in 1972, playing 46 matches including the Haig and Petersfield knockouts. On 7 May the club, who had a friendly home fixture against Steep, were drawn against East Tytherley in the Haig competition on the same day! Fortunately the draw was away and Hambledon succeeded in raising two teams, and in defeating East Tytherley. In the next round Steep were the opposition. So 18 June saw them again putting out two sides simultaneously.

Ron Turner stood down as captain at the AGM in February 1973, though, mercifully, he continued as hon. secretary. Topsy Turner was elected in his place. Ron commented that the emergence of league cricket had somewhat hampered the arranging of friendly fixtures, but he had filled all Saturdays bar two for 1973. The side still did well in competitive cricket, even though they were not as yet in the league. In 1974 they reached the semi-final of the evening league, which was by then known as the Strong Cup, but that autumn the committee decided, narrowly by four votes to two, not to enter the Haig competition in 1975 "unless changes in the rules warranted consideration." By way of elaboration Ron Turner told the AGM that they had decided to withdraw because of fixture problems (arising perhaps from the necessity to raise two teams at the same time), and because changes in the rules were necessary to promote the Haig as a true village competition. Competition rules also played a part in the disappearance of the club that year from the Petersfield Knock-out. After defeating Headley in the semi-final Hambledon were reported for infringement of a regulation which limited players taking part in later rounds to those participating in rounds one and two, even though the players involved were club members and regular players. That even the organisers found that the rule was harsh was shown when they modified it before the next season.

From the mid 70s the club found that they had very few opponents below their own standard and their seasons figures usually showed victories only just exceeding defeats: in 1972 by 19 to 18; in 1973 by 18 to 14, and in 1974 by 14 to 12. When they could put their best team out, as they usually did in competition matches, they were a powerful combination particularly in bowling. R. Munton, L. Marchant, J. James, E. Chaplin, A. Mason, Colin Barrett, J. Banting and J. Thompson all produced fine analyses, but still the outstanding all-rounder was Topsy Turner right hand bat and off spin bowler and his figures over the seasons show his consistent all round excellence:

Year	Runs	Batting Ave.	Wickets	Bowling Ave.
1969	667	35.1	69	10.55
1970	937	36	NO FIGURES	
1971		NO FIGURES AVAILABLE		
1972	583	24	60	11.01
1973	538	31	27	14.44
1974	1031	44.82	82	11.93
1975	1032	27.15	100	13.39

His batting figures in 1974 have been unsurpassed in the history of the club, and his achievement of the double feat in 1975 remains unique. Both seasons' performances earned him a special award from the club but he had and has plenty more to contribute yet.

Colin Barrett excelled with 848 runs in 1973 and 808 two years later when, by then an inspiring captain of the club, he also claimed 50 wickets. Dave Dunham hit up over 600 runs in 1970 and 1972, as did J. Anthony in the latter year.

At the AGM in 1976 when the members voted to re-enter the Haig competition in 1977 (but the application was made too late, and they had to wait a year), Ken Moon reported the first financial loss for years, but the club still had over £1000 in hand. He drew the members' attention to the cost of ground maintenance on which they had spent over £300 in the previous year by employing a part time groundsman with varying results. In 1976 the committee decided to have electricity supplied to the pavilion as part of a programme of renovation and extension, with the promise of support from the brewers Ind Coope. It is a measure of the rate of inflation in the 70s that Alan Mason's estimate for the work on the pavilion which he placed at over £6000 was twice the cost of the original construction work seven years before.

The new structural work cost £3000, plumbing £665, the installation of electricity £1342 and fittings £505. Mr. Sykes readily gave his consent and the extension was completed in 1979, the new bar doubling up as a tea preparation and service area: a great improvement for the hard working caterers.

A further good idea from Desmond Eagar led to more fundraising when he suggested to the club chairman Charles Lutyens that the club celebrate a bi-centenary of importance in its history with a match in June 1977. It celebrated the occasion in 1777 when Hambledon scored 403 and beat England by an innings and 168 runs. James Aylward scored 167 between 5pm on the Wednesday and 3pm on the following Friday. Both the team's total and Aylward's phenomenal score were records, yet as Desmond Eager pointed out in the match brochure Aylward was defending a third stump which had only lately been added under the laws. That year had seen Hambledon at the height of its fame.

Originally contemplated as an old-fashioned style match against HMS Mercury, the game played at Broadhalfpenny Down developed into a modern day contest against a strong MCC side with Mercury contributing two players to the Hambledon team, in return for the naval station's assistance with preparations on the ground for what it was correctly anticipated would attract a very large crowd. A year's preparation went into the arrangements: the hire of marquees, provision of parking in the neighbouring fields, and a search for sponsorship. In this Christopher Bazalgette who was co-opted onto the committee proved invaluable: he designed the match brochure, secured ample advertising and generally publicised the event. Charles Lutyens laid on lunch for the players before the match, and John Goldsmith was on hand to provide a loudspeaker commentary. Ind Coope promised £200 and a trophy, while Domeque also offered £200 for the man of the match award and provided food and drink after the match. Winchester College for the first time agreed to charges being made at the gate. BBC South wished to make a short feature film about four of the Hambledon players and to film extracts from the match. 10,000 tickets were printed and by mid June advance sales of programmes and advertising amounted to over £1000. On 11 July part of the committee meeting which was devoted to the match arrangements was filmed by BBC TV.

The profits of the match on 31 July were in the region of £1700, and the club awarded life membership to Chris Bazalgette. I well

CHAPTER 15

Hambledon v All England in 1977.
Back row: Roy Newman, Adrian Magrath, Peter Tomkins, Mark Wingham, Greg Murton. Middle row: Freddy Millett, Brian Hamblyn, Mike Griffith, Jack Miller, Robert Turner, Steve Horn, Alan Mason, Chris Bazalgette. Front. Ted Clark, Dudley Owen-Thomas, John Lofting, Michael Mence, Colin Barrett, Charles Fry, Jack Bailey, Colin Cowdrey, Alan Day, Steve Sims.

remember that brilliant summer day, the crowd basking in deckchairs or in several rows on the grass enjoying the presence on the field of a strong MCC side led by J.A. Bailey, of Oxford and Essex, who was later the secretary of MCC, whose team included Colin Cowdrey, Ted Clark of Middlesex, Charles Fry of Repton, Oxford and Hampshire, and grandson of C.B., M.G. Griffith of Marlborough, Cambridge and Sussex, and last, but by no means least, Colin Milburne the Northants and England player whose first class career had been ended by loss of an eye in a car crash.

The Hambledon side was Colin Barrett, Chris Bazalgette, S. Horn, Alan Mason, A. Magrath, J. Miller, G. Munton, R. Newman, D. Stephenson, Peter Tomkins, Topsy Turner and Mark Wingham. Topsy Turner was man of the match.

It was not surprising that the committee eagerly embraced a further match in 1978 against a Hampshire County side for the benefit of the Hampshire captain Richard Gilliat. In the event they raised a good sum for him, but there was not quite the same enthusiasm among the public for this repeat performance. Moreover the club lacked the energy

*Colin Barrett (front row centre) with his team which won the
County round of the village knock-out at Longparish in 1977.
Back row (left to right): Charles Lutyens, Bill Enstone,
Alan Mason, Peter Tomkins, Dave Dunham, Adrian Magrath, Steve Horn.
Front: Mark Wingham, Jack Miller, Robert Turner, Danny Stephenson.*

and support of Desmond Eagar, who had died suddenly following an operation in the previous September. His loss was mourned by numerous friends and organisations and his charm, energy and activity were sorely missed. Hambledon had by then also lost the services of Ron Turner, whose long and admirable stint as hon. secretary came to an end with his retirement at the AGM in March 1977, 46 years after his father had first taken over the post. Business commitments were the reason for his departure. The club showed their appreciation by presenting him with a handsome cheque; they had already made a gift to him of a briefcase a year or two before. Colin Barrett was elected to succeed him and at the AGM in 1978 Cecil Paris became President. So at a time of strength when the new secretary had to have 200 fixture cards printed for members and vice presidents, Hambledon could look forward with confidence.

Chapter 16
Success in the Leagues

"The coldest Good Friday this century", as one participant put it, saw members at work on the pavilion. As early as mid March 1983 everything was in order and ready for the new season, following the successful climax of the previous year when the club gained promotion in the Hampshire League for the second year in succession, up to Division 2. After 10 years as a wise counsellor in the chair, Charles Lutyens retired; on his marriage in June the club presented him with two flowering shrubs. He was succeeded by Bob Beagley.

The ground now boasted first rate covers for the square, constructed by Steve Sims, and they were described as truly magnificent and the envy of other clubs. The timing of their arrival could not have been bettered, as after a good victory over Bass Alton, which brought the club 21 points, five games out of the following seven were rained off, followed by two further wash outs before mid June.

On Bank Holiday Monday a side composed of under 25s beat their seniors by 98 runs to 89. Those involved included Topsy Turner, Adrian Magrath, Mark Wingham, Chris de Mellow, Mike de Mellow, Mike Donaldson, Mark Le Clercq, Colin Barrett, Richard Jones, G. Faithful, Ian Turner, R. Hall, Ian Barrett, A. Murphy, Ian Beagley, G. Pask, Peter Tomkins, and Steve Sims. That season did not bring further promotion although Colin Barrett told the AGM in October 1983 that advance into Division 1 could not be far away. With this typically optimistic comment which proved absolutely accurate he announced his retirement from the captaincy which he had held for nine years: a glutton for punishment he remained in office as secretary; the debt which the club owed him as an inspiring and dynamic leader, and one of the finest all-rounders the club ever had cannot be overstated. As secretary he continued to extend the fixture list: in the autumn of 1985 he proposed to arrange and organise mid-week cricket with matches taking place on Mondays, Tuesdays and Thursdays principally against tourists and, true to his word, by October had 37 such fixtures on his list.

Meanwhile in 1984 he achieved the double feat of scoring 1000 runs and taking 100 wickets, which had previously been achieved for the club only by Topsy Turner. It is a matter for debate whether 1984, or 1989, has been the clubs most glorious summer. In the former season the 1st XI led by Chris de Mellow gained promotion to Division 1 of the league, while the Seconds won the South Down League in its inaugural year. Rolf Munro Hall became the youngest player in the clubs history to score a century and Bob White also reached three figures. The successful 2nd XI captain Peter Tomkins carried his bat for 60 against the Brigands. Adrian Magrath won the batting award and Christopher Bazalgette was the most successful bowler.

The truly significant development for the club came about before the season even started. The decision had been taken to extend the pavilion once more, and the round of fundraising made a successful beginning. Bob Beagley approached Mr. Sykes the ground landlord for his approval to the development. Mr. Sykes said he had no objection but then came the bombshell as he added that he wished to sell the ground to the club. He had already purchased the land from Winchester College. After some deliberation the price was agreed at £2500. So the great prize fell into the clubs hands, or more formally, into the hands of their trustees, Geoffrey Hartridge, Ron Turner and Charles Lutyens with completion of the purchase taking place in September 1985. Mr. Sykes' offer acted as a spur to fundraising: individual donations realised £1500, Hampshire Playing Fields granted £1000, as did the Sports Council, the Parish Council talked of making a gift and Hartridges made an interest-free loan.

Typical of the enthusiasm of those heady days were the efforts of Maureen Barrett, whose "buy a brick" scheme and car washing during matches raised well over £250 and of Bob Beagley whose letters to the great and the good produced a four-figure sum. A further extension to the pavilion was complete in time for the season of 1985 and Mr. Salvati, the club solicitor had obtained a bar license by July. Hambledon indeed, with their enhanced fixture list, league commitments, fundraising functions and themselves now acting as a landlord letting the ground in winter to the hockey club, and with the benefit of its bar, was becoming more and more like a trading organisation and the time had come to spread the administrative load. The committee set up three further sub committees - there was already a selection sub committee - for the bar, fundraising, ground and pavilion. Colin Barrett was appointed to two of them, bar and ground, but early in 1986 he had to give up the secretaryship because of increased work commitments. These did not prevent him leading Hambledon's 2nd XI in his usual inspiring fashion to promotion from SE Hants League Division 2.

Chris de Mellow, after two successful seasons as captain also had to resign because of work commitments, but he stood in for Colin, first on an interim basis then permanently as hon. secretary. Steve "Fods" Faithful was elected first team captain. The new skipper quickly expressed his concern about the number of club members who were available to play, in proportion to the fixtures and the committee gave him the go ahead to advertise for players in the Evening News. Soon the problem crystallised: like many other clubs with league commitments on Saturdays Hambledon found it increasingly difficult to raise sides for friendly fixtures on Sundays, and the committee agreed to prune the lists. There were now winter fixtures too and in 1985-86 Topsy Turner and his team won the Waterlooville indoor league.

1986 was described as a disappointing season as the club finished as low as 12th in the league, but there were memorable moments, or rather episodes, like Chris de Mellow's 98 and Topsy Turner's eight wickets which led to a great win over Hungerford. Mark le Clercq won the batting award and yet again Topsy Turner with his son Ian, slow left arm, at the other end, displayed his skill and stamina. Lloyd Hall however was awarded the bowling trophy. The year ended with a burst of fundraising, the annual jumble sale which realised £177, a race night £160, and Mrs. Lutyens Christmas Fair from which she donated £200. Maureen Barrett crowned the year with a successful club Christmas Dinner.

Tony Baker, who had succeeded Cecil Paris as President, was the first winner of the new 75 club draw organised by Mark Wingham. The winner of the second prize was Mark Wingham! The club received a small but welcome windfall in the form of a legacy from Austin McKay Reilly, a resident of Scotland, of whom none of the committee had ever heard.

At this time the club became, from the financial point of view, a victim of its own success. They ran the weekend and league matches but in addition there were, in 1987, 49 midweek games and it proved increasingly difficult to keep track of the bar stocks and sales. At length the club accounts were in the red and the hon. treasurer called on the committee to take further control. The club like many others was finding how difficult it was to reconcile in the broadest sense the stock, sales, and percentage turnover of alcoholic liquors. They returned to their best form in the field, or rather on the mat, winning the Alton Indoor League Division 2 at the end of the winter, and both the 1st and 2nd XIs finished sixth in their respective leagues. The firsts also reached the final of the Noel Fisher Knock-out, where they lost narrowly to Longparish. (However they won the trophy the following year). It was perhaps in retrospect a benefit that the number of midweek games was greatly reduced as Colin Barrett had been offered the job of groundsman at Warnford, the home of the Hampshire Hogs. On the credit side his friends congratulated Ian Turner on joining the staff at the County Ground where he was the first Hambledon player to be offered a contract, and he became the first to play for the County since Edward Whalley-Tooker in 1882. He still found time to strengthen the attack taking 55 wickets, to Topsy Turners 40. Steve Faithful also excelled. Outstanding in batting were Mark le Clercq and Greg Small, an Australian and the club's first overseas star. For the 2nd XI, which Colin Barrett felt should have done better, Greg Carson averaged over 50, and Peter Tomkins more than 30.

For the season of 1988 the captains were, for the 1st XI Mike Donaldson, and the 2nd Phil Campbell. The season began with a departure when the committee received a letter from Colin Barrett resigning from his remaining office within the club, that of fixture secretary. His flair and energy would be sadly missed, but the loss was mitigated by the appointment of Mike de Mellow in his place. Not all secretaries impart their personality to their club's minutes, but Colin certainly did: for example in June 1983: after a well meant offer of help "we are now waiting in anticipation, and baited breath as to his next move..."

July 1983 "Judges XI. Desire of skipper that all the committee play as token of their hard work. Naturally all agreed. Democracy at work."

1 April 1985 (the committee decided to cancel the game on 4 May on the ground that it was Cup Final day) "the hon. sec cancelled the match with Northwood IOW. However he did have it pointed out by Northwood's secretary that 4 May was not the Cup Final..."

October 1985 on the formation of the bar sub committee: "after one or two hiccups it is running smoothly."

No wonder Brian Johnston meeting Colin while recording for Down Your Way, the well known radio programme, was so enchanted with his conversation that the interview might have gone on all day, had the producer not separated them.

Chapter 17
Natural Popular Favourites

In 1989, the year the Berlin Wall came down, and Australia won the Ashes by four tests to nil in spite of the efforts of Robin Smith, who averaged 61 for England power driving centuries at Manchester and Nottingham, while Worcestershire were County Champions largely because the runners up Essex were penalised 25 points for a sub standard pitch at Southend

HAMBLEDON WENT TO LORDS

in the final of the National Village Championship.

The tension of this near-triumph built up gradually through the early, local Hampshire, rounds, when Hambledon knocked out Amport and Hursley in turn, John Barrett's 67 not out in the first match and Mark le Clercq's 128 against Hursley being the chief contributory factors. The off spin of Topsy Turner who took four wickets at the negligible cost of 13 runs led to victory over Sparsholt in the Hampshire semi-final. Excitement really set in as Hambledon faced Longparish, the village champions of 1987, to decide which of them should go through to the national rounds. As Mike Donaldson, the Hambledon captain has written, games against Longparish the "auld enemy" were always tense affairs and this one was a nail-biter, with brothers Mike and Chris de Mellow adding 40 at a crisis point to ensure that Hambledon overhauled a score of 173, with three wickets in hand.

Poynings, the first opponents in the national rounds were beaten with welcome ease by 90 runs, Adrian "Mac" Magrath making the chief contribution to the winning total of 225 for 6. It was not to be so easy again: travelling to Linton Park, near Maidstone, Hambledon hit up 185 for 6 in front of what Mike describes as a partisan crowd, who then saw their heroes advance by fits and starts until 13 were needed from the final over which was to be delivered by Steve Faithful. His first ball sailed back over the bowler's head for six, but he kept his nerve conceding only one run from the next three balls. Six to lose - a would-be sharp single off the fifth ball led to a run out, from a direct hit by the bowler, and so to a win for Hambledon. In the quarter-final they beat Hordon-On-The-Hill, near Southend, by ten wickets, thanks to John Brindley's bag of five wickets for 24, Colin Pay's score of 59 and Mark le Clercq's 46.

Both these games had drawn sizeable crowds, but the semi-final at Ridge Meadow at a time when the clubs successes in the competition had attracted affectionate nation-wide publicity drew a record number of spectators estimated at over 3000. Hambledon's opponents, St. Fagans from South Wales made their hosts struggle to a less than imposing total of 139 to which Colin Pay contributed 33. The Welshmen responded by despatching the Hambledon openers to all quarters with 36 from the first four overs. Hambledon had to draw on all the fighting qualities which made them so formidable in that memorable summer. A brilliant catch by Chris de Mellow proved the turning point although the turn was slow. The middle 20 overs yielded only 27 runs while five wickets fell to Topsy Turner and Mike Donaldson with two scalps each. The visitors' last wicket fell in the final over when they were still eight runs short.

It was a fine achievement in front of that large demonstrative and happy crowd; ahead loomed media exposure and the lure of a Lords final, against Toft. Hambledon were, as Wisden described them, natural popular favourites. Every well constructed story has its climax, but although Mike Donaldson and his men did not know it the climax was to last until the team had arrived expectantly at the home of cricket only to disperse when after Mike won the toss Hambledon batted. In 29 overs they scored 72 while five wickets fell, only Mark le Clercq with a total of 33 really making any headway before rain caused an abandonment. Relief on the one hand and frustration on the other were not allowed to last long. The match was replayed the next day at the Midland Bank Ground at Beckenham, because Lords was unavailable. Hambledon again batted first but this time because Alan Stimpson of Toft won the toss and put them in. They were bowled out in 37 overs on a drying pitch for 104. The effects of the heavy roller suited Colin Pay who, bowling very fast and moving the ball, cheaply dismissed both openers, but the effect soon wore off, and an unbroken fifth wicket stand of 40 saw Toft home with five overs to spare.

As Wisden put it "victory at Lords is the essential objective of club and village finalists" and losing had not been on Hambledon's agenda. Let Mike have the last word: "We had seemed untouchable. We were now numbed by the harsh reality of defeat, but for all that I believe Toft were the better side on both days."

Hambledon at Lords in the Final of the National Village Championship 1989,

Hambledon
C. Pay st. Wood b. Locke 8
M.A. Le Clercq c. Coutts b. Locke 7
A.H. Magrath c. Coutts b. Locke 1
S. James c. Caro b. Coutts 37
M.G. de Mellow c. Wood b. Challenor ... 1
J. Barrett c. Stimpson b. Challenor 7
*M.J. Donaldson c. Wood b. Challenor .. 0
C.J. de Mellow c. and b. Caro 2
J.M. Brindley c. Stimpson b. Coutts 20
S. Faithful b. Challenor 2
R.J. Turner not out 3
    L-b 9, w 5, n-b 2 16

1/8 2/11 3/25   (37 overs)   104
4/29 5/41 6/48
7/56 8/89 9/101

Bowling: Locke 9-5-11-3; Bertenshaw 9-1-17-0; Challenor 8-1-32-4; Caro 7-0-19-1; Coutts 4-0-16-2

Toft

*A. Stimpson c. James b. Pay 3
S. Turner c. Turner b. Pay 0
A. Caro not out 37
D. Stiles c. Faithful b. Pay 10
R. Ashley c. Barrett b. Turner 17
R. Burke not out 19
    B 6, l-b 3, w 10 19

1/4 2/5 (4 wkts, 35 overs)   105
3/31 4/65

A. Gibson, L. Challenor, B. Coutts,
S. Wood and P. Bertenshaw did not bat

Bowling: Pay 8-1-31-3; Faithful 9-1-15-0;
Turner 9-1-20-1; Donaldson 6-2-17-0;
Brindley 3-0-13-0

Umpires: K.T. Francis and C.T. Puckett

* * *

There have been other triumphs in the 1990s, even if the trip to Lords has not yet been repeated.

The other significant event of 1989 was Ian Turner's successful debut for Hampshire against Glamorgan at the seasons end. Described by Wisden as bowling with commendable common sense and flighting the ball well, Ian achieved the following figures in the two innings.

    18 overs, 8 maidens, 28 runs, 1 wicket
    and
    17 overs, 13 maidens, 20 runs, 3 wickets

which gave genuine pleasure both at Hambledon and at the County Ground.

CHAPTER 18

Nervous Nineties

In February 1989 Ron Turner died after a short illness, his loss being all the more greatly felt as it occurred at a comparatively early age. He and his father between them had served the club in the post of secretary for 46 years and he had long been a leading member of the side as well as serving as captain. He left the club a substantial legacy and later in the year, in the euphoria following the club's trip to Lords, there was talk of some sort of memorial to him, possibly to consist of a further enlargement of the pavilion. The proposal - particularly the money side of it - rather divided the membership into two factions, those with a sense of what was practicable and those without. Nothing was done for some time until matters came to a head at the AGM in 1993. Bob Beagley stood down after 10 successful and eventful years in the chair and the vote for his successor turned into a referendum on the pavilion question. Peter Tomkins, who had been a member of the side for many years and urged financial prudence, was defeated by the candidate who favoured the building campaign. The immediate result was that Peter left the club and went on to set up a rival organisation. In the longer term his successful opponent, while desiring success for Hambledon, had no great familiarity with the club or its set-up. When he stood down after two seasons, there had been little development in regard to the pavilion, except the delivery of the architect's bill.

Then there was the occasion of the Old England match in 1994 when the caterers arrived only to find another company in possession of the field or rather the kitchen...
Chris de Mellow was elected chairman at the AGM in November 1995 and continued until the AGM this year.

The club has met with varying fortunes over the last decade. Their success in the 80s led them to anticipate a further raising of standards when they entered the Southern League in 1992 after winning Division 1 of the County League. In fact the best position they achieved was sixth in the 1994 season, and it was only by a whisker that they twice avoided relegation through events unconnected with performance on the field. Finishing last in 1997, they were saved when the Trojans dropped out because of defective conditions at their ground; in the following season the turn of fate again enabled them to stay up, when

Playing in 1994 alongside former England skipper David Gower, who captained Hambledon in a match against an Old England XI. Back row (left to right): Matt Jones, Robert Turner, Steve Faithfull, Mike de Mellow, Iain Beagley, Andy James, Phil Campbell, John Burdekin, Pete Wood, John Barrett, Terry Wood. Sitting: Simon Clapham, Mike Donaldson, Simon James, David Gower, Graham Smith, Chris de Mellow.

United Services, Portsmouth were ejected through their failure to develop a colts side. In truth Hambledon's opponents in the Southern League were from a higher class of club cricket, and the side never quite came to terms with the likes of Bournemouth, Havant and South Wilts. In 1999, following a restructuring of the league, Hambledon entered the second division but they still remain among the top twenty clubs in the region.

Entry into the Southern League caused a more direct disappointment as it resulted in the club ceasing to qualify for the Cricketer Village Knock-Out in which they had been so successful, as the league was a "cross border competition" whose participants were ineligible for the Cricketer contests. So, like Usk in 2000, they were "knocked out" on a technicality. It was little compensation at the time that Hambledon's old rivals St. Fagan suffered the same fate.

The team were however Noel Fisher finalists in 1991, as they had been in 1981 and 1987 and the second XI finished on top of the South East Hants League in 1990. Four years later they earned promotion to Division 5 of the Hampshire League, and soon promoted to Division 4, headed that too in 1996.

To set against these successes came the tragedy of the sudden death of Colin Barrett while on tour in the midlands in 1991. This born leader had held almost every office in the club and been involved in every aspect of its activity, as preceding chapters have shown. As a captain he had the ability to turn the direction of a game to his teams advantage, and to make each member of his side feel that he had a contribution to make. His charisma enthusiasm and energy both on and off the field were luminous.

The 90s saw the arrival of other sponsored overseas players following Greg Small through the clubs contact with Harry Solomon the Sydney sports retailer. The present incumbent, another welcome arrival is Bret van Deinsen, who has had first class experience with New South Wales.

The club also decided to establish a colts section around 1990, and it has become a highly significant development. At the present time more than 70 children, boys and girls, are trained by qualified coaches: youngsters are welcome from the age of seven when they are introduced to kwik cricket and so develop up through the various formal age groups at under 11, 13 and 15 years. All three of these age groups play in the South East Hants cricket league and the club is now well represented at each age at district level. As the older boys move up to the under 15 squad, Mike de Mellow believes that they will make an impact at all three district levels. An under 12 team competed last winter in the outdoor winter league at Portsmouth's Mountbatten Centre, finishing equal top with two other teams in a league of eight.

As noted in Chapter 1, the club runs three teams at adult level as well as a ladies side which was due to play 27 matches in 2000, most of them in the National League involving teams from as far afield as Cambridge and Shepperton. In 1999, their maiden year, Claire Slaney's side achieved 17 victories, won the Hampshire League title, and gained promotion from National League Division 3 South East, to Division 2 South. They also won the Hampshire six-a-side tournament and in the National Plate lost only to the eventual winners, Brighton and Hove. Seven senior and two junior members played for the county: Lorna Jesty, daughter of Trevor, the former Hampshire all-rounder and England one day International, was selected for winter training for England.

This ladies team has already produced one century maker in vice-captain Marina Steel, whose 440 runs, average 36 in 1999, found her at the top of the batting averages, while Becky Rowe led the bowling with 24 victims and conceded under two runs an over. Jacqueline Turner, daughter of Topsy, at the age of 17, plays for Hampshire Under 19s.

The club still sets its sights on Broadhalfpenny Down, not

withstanding the high quality of the amenities at Brook Lane. In 1992 they competed unsuccessfully when Winchester College invited bids for a new lease of the ground. As far as the club were concerned, the successful tenderers, Broadhalfpenny Brigands at this juncture lived up to their name! Hambledon's interest is at present limited to eight games a season for their third XI on the hallowed turf. Even this helps to reduce the demands on the square at Ridge Meadow, which result from the heavy fixture list. In 2000, 47 games were played there. Previously the third XI were despatched to King George's Playing Fields, Winchester for some of their home fixtures.

The season of 2000 was a particularly busy one, with its anniversary cricket week, and a game with Lord Alexander's other club, MCC, as well as a game with Old England.

In the week, the scores were:

v. Dartford 12.6.2000
Dartford 224 for 6
Hambledon 170 for 9
J. Snowdon scored 65 for Dartford
M. Wingham scored 60 for Hambledon

v. Slindon 13.6.2000
Hambledon 250 for 2
Slindon 215 for 8
R. Kenway scored 132 not out for Hambledon
G. Shotton scored 82
Bowling: W. Norman age 12: 5 wickets for 28

v. Chertsey 14.6.2000
Hambledon 233 for 8
Chertsey 140 all out
D. Carson scored 155 for Hambledon

v. Caterham 15.6.2000
Caterham 210 for 9
Hambledon 166 all out
M. de Mellow scored 49 for Hambledon
J. Vaughn-Davis scored 86 for Caterham
R. Chapman 4 wickets for 60 for Caterham

v. Farnham 16.6.2000
Hambledon 254 for 4
K. Otiena scored 90
C. Pay scored 37
D. Carson scored 50 not out
Stedman scored 88
Farnham 237 for 6

v. Sevenoaks Vine 18.6.2000
Hambledon 195 for 1
D. Carson scored 81
R. Norris scored 92 not out
Sevenoaks Vine 198 for 4
S. Sherreff scored 87 not out for Sevenoaks

The season ended with a match against Old England at Ridge Meadow on 10 September. After Old England had declared at 179 for four, to which Roger Tolchard, the former Leicestershire and England wicketkeeper/batsman, contributed a stylish 54, Hambledon were left a little over 90 minutes to get the runs yet they fell only 16 short with five wickets left. David Carson, the club's Australian professional led the charge, immediately hitting Essex and England fast bowler John Lever to the boundary and later took 19 off one over delivered by the Kent and England spinner Derek Underwood. Local hero Robert Norris made a rapid 40 before he too fell to a catch in the deep off Underwood.

As to 2000 as a whole, Marion Beagley writes "It has been quite a good season really; the weather early on did nothing for a few matches but all three teams avoided relegation worries and in fact two of them did very well indeed.

First XI - Won 7, lost 8. Ended 5th in the league table out of 10 teams and will stay in Division 2 of the ECB Southern Premier League.

Second XI - Won 4, lost 11. Ended 14th out of 17 in the Hants County Division 2 league table and will stay there next season. They will need to strengthen the team next year.

Third XI - Won 8, lost 4. Ended 6th out of 18 teams in the Hants Combination, Eastern Division where they will stay. This was quite an achievement by the third team, very often short of players as the 2nd team had to take players to make up their numbers. Congratulations should go to Phil Tusler for his hard work.

The Anniversary matches have now ended with a really splendid day at Ridge Meadow on 10th September against Old England. The weather was marvellous, there was a good crowd of spectators, and the Old England team really did consist of many famous names from the recent past. The match was drawn but that did not matter.

The match against the ex-Hampshire players was spoiled by rain at tea time, and therefore ended as a draw. It was, however, an enjoyable day for all concerned.

The three Colts teams have had a good season and thanks are due to Mike de Mellow and his assistants for the organisation of the Colts. The under 11s played 9 and won 4 of them; the under 13s played 12 and won 6; and the under 15s played 8 and won 2; these were more difficult games and the 3rd team occasionally borrowed a Colt to make up numbers."

1997 saw the first appearance for Hampshire of another Hambledon product, Derek Kenway. Within two years he had completed 1000 runs in a first class season, aged 21, at the high average of 42, with a maiden century against Warwickshire at Southampton; details which are highly impressive. This year, one of some agitation for county supporters, he has put together the considerable total of 136, the second highest score ever made by a Hampshire wicket-keeper (he was deputising for the injured Adie Aymes) and then claimed five victims behind the stumps to equal Bobby Parks' Sunday League record for the county against Derbyshire, and his opportunities, like his enthusiasm, seem limitless.

As many as 16 of the current members have reached three figures at various levels and, as to achieve a century remains a mark of distinction their names should be recorded.

John Burdekin	102* v. Findon 1994
Phil Campbell	143* v.
	100* v. Burridge. This led to the side winning the S.E. Hants Division 1 title.
Indy Chakrabati	105 v. Philanderers
Mike Donaldson	100* v. Hook and Newnham. Chasing 252 to win, Hambledon won by nine wickets.
Simon James	163 v. Chandlers Ford
Matt Jones	101

Mannish Khurana	134 v. Havant, County Division 3 in 1999
Mark le Clercq	151* in Hants League Division 1 128* v. Hursley in the village knockout 1989.
Adrian Magrath	152* v. Longparish
Gary Shotton	124*
Allan Smith	111 v. Hungerford 2nds
Marina Steel	114* v. Lymington in the Hampshire League
Ian Turner	177 v. Havant 3rds
Robert Turner	127: his achievements are celebrated. See for example Chapter 15.
Phil Tusler	101* v. Crondall 1996
Mark Wingham	159*. Mark has hit 17 centuries for Hambledon but he regards as his greatest piece of batting his 50 v. Hungerford off 36 balls.

What would Richard Nyren have thought of it all? He would be proud, to have been succeeded, not by so many heads and right arms, which has the aspect of an accident and emergency department, but by loyal supporters of the club like J.A. Best, Edward Whalley-Tooker, Burton F.J. Cooper, J.E. Turner, Ron Turner and Colin Barrett, of those who have gone before, and played their part in ensuring that Hambledon Cricket Club has achieved the status it has today.

The season of 2000 could not have begun earlier as Hambledon greeted what has been described as the New Millennium with a match with Adie Aymes XI beginning at midnight on 1 January when one ball was bowled in the glare of car headlights.

The ten-overs-a-side match resumed at noon on a glorious sparkling day, which, windless, showed Broadhalfpenny Down at its best, the bare trees and long views accentuating the sense of timelessness which overcomes any visitor with a feeling for history and the passing of the generations. The monument and The Bat and Ball, timeless, looked on.

Officers of the Club

President
1878 A. Arnold
1879 Capt. T.D. Butler
 (later Sir Thomas
 Butler KCVO)
1938 Edward Whalley-
 Tooker
1941 Mrs. D. Whalley-
 Tooker
1962 E.D.R. Eager
1978 C.G.A. Paris
1986 A.F. Baker
1996 Lord Alexander of
 Weedon Q.C.

Captain
1878 A. Arnold
? - 1895 E.F.W. Lunn
1896 E. Whalley-Tooker
1937 C. Chesterfield
1939 Revd A.C. Champion
1946 F. Banting
1947 W.G. Tanner
1948 F. Banting
1951 W.G. Tanner
1952 R.J. Turner
1958 F. Hall
1959 R. Beagley
1962 F. Hall
1963 R.J. Turner
1973 Robert Turner
1974 J. Banting
1975 C. Barrett
1984 C. de Mellow
1986 S. Faithful
1987 M. Donaldson
1990 M. Le Clercq
1994 S. James
1995 Kelvan Finch
1996 S. James
1997 R. Kenway
2000 I. Turner

Hon. Secretary
1864 Sidney Lunn
1878 J.A. Best
1882 F. Crook
? - 1894 Edgar Lunn
1897 J.A. Best
1906 H.A. Grant
1906 Revd H. Floud
1911 Burton F.J. Cooper
1926 F. Macey
1931 J.E. Turner
1960 R.J. Turner
1976 C. Barrett
1986 C. de Mellow
1996 Marion Beagley

Hon. Treasurer
1878 W. Walter
1882 E. Goldsmith
? - 1895 E.P. Durrant
1898 J.A. Best
1906 H.J. Allin
1906 Revd H. Floud
1911 Burton F.J. Cooper
1923 E.F. Wren
1926 A. Hall
1958 K. Moon
1977 W. Enstone
1990 R.J. Donaldson

Chairman
1864 – 1961
Elected at each meeting
  1961 J.W. Hall
  1964 L. Lilley
1969 J.W. Hall
1973 C. Lutyens
1982 R. Beagley
1993 T. Wood
1995 C. de Mellow

Books and Documents Consulted

Aesop. *Sporting Reminiscences of Hampshire from 1745 to 1862.* Chapman & Hall 1864

Anon. Booklet commemorating the All-England match in September 1908

H.S. Altham. Dates in cricket history, and costume, from Wisden's Cricketers' Almanack 1964

F.S. Ashley-Cooper. *The Hambledon Cricket Chronicle*, Herbert Jenkins 1924: His personal scrapbook of Hambledon material

William Cobbett. *Rural Rides*

David Frith. *Pageant of Cricket*, Macmillan London 1987

Fred Gale. *The Game of Cricket*, 2nd Edition, Swan Sonnenschein & Lowrey 1888

Norman Gannaway. *A History of Cricket in Hampshire*, Hampshire Books 1990

John Goldsmith. *Hambledon*, Phillimore & Co Ltd, 1994

Hambledon Cricket Club Millennium Souvenir The Club 2000

Vivienne Hughes and James Lord. *Hambledon 2000* Record of the village. Hambledon Millennium Committee

Arthur Haygarth. Scores and Biographies Volumes I, II and III The Oval, Kennington, Lillywhite 1862-63, Volume VIII Longmans, 1877

Kelly's Directories Various dates

Ronald D. Knight. *Hambledon's Cricket Glory*, Various dates, Weymouth, Bat & Ball Press

E.V. Lucas. *The Hambledon Men*, Frowde 1907

– 151 –

Col. John May. *Cricket in North Hants Basingstoke*, Warren 1906

Ashley Mote. *The Glory Days of Cricket*, Robson Books London 1997

Terry Norman. *Journeys to Yesterday* – Hambledon

John Nyren. *The Young Cricketers Tutor and The Cricketers of My Time* – Edited by Ashley Mote, Robson Books London 1998

E.W. Padwick. *A Bibliography of Cricket.* Second Edition, The Library Association, 1984

The Rev James Pycroft. *The Cricket Field*, Edited by F.S. Ashley-Cooper, St. James' Press 1922

E.E. Snow. *Accounts of the Earl of Winchilsea*, Journal of The Cricket Society, Autumn 1976, p.26, Spring 1977, p.35

H.F. and A.P. Squire. *Pre-Victorian Sussex Cricket*, Henfield 1971

Thomas Smith. *Sporting Incidents in the Life of Another Tom Smith*, Chapman & Hall 1867

White. *Directory of Hampshire 1859*

Who's Who 1928, A. & C. Black

Philip Bailey, Philip Thorn & Peter Wynne-Thomas. *Who's Who of Cricketers*, London 1982

Wisden's Cricketers Almanack 1909, 1964, and 1990

Hambledon Cricket Club. The Steward's Notebook, Scorebooks, Minute Books and Fixture Cards as listed in Appendix

Bob Beagley. File of Correspondence

APPENDIX

List of Scorebooks, Minute Books, Fixture Cards and Averages

Scorebooks	**Minute Books**	1928
1864 – 1869	1857 – 1863	1930
1884	1878 – 1882	1931
1891	1894	1934
1900 – 1901	1895 – 1907	1946
1905 – 1906	1907 – 1940	1947
1907 – 1908	1940 – 1951	1960
1908 – 1909	1951 – 1960	1995 to date
War Years	1961 – 1978	
1924 – 1925	1979 – 1990	**Averages**
1931 – 1932	1991 – 1995	1905
1933 – 1936		1906, 1907, 1909
1936 – 1937	**Fixture Cards**	1911
1937 – 1938	1911	1914
1938 – 1940	1919	1923
War Years	1925	1924
1946 – 1947	1926	1931

Index

101st Regiment of Fusiliers 34
22nd Regiment R.A. 97
36/55 Battery 97
52nd Light Infantry 36
53rd Regiment 34

A

Abel, Bobby 57
Abinett 20
Adderley, Captain 44
Aird, Ronald 124
All-England match 63
Allen, J. 52
Allin, H.J. 64, 66
Altham, Harry
 37, 77, 106, 119, 120
Amos, A. 72
Ancient Firemen's match 112
Anthony, J. 131
Arlott, John 119
Arnold, A. 38, 42, 43
Arnold, W.J. 78
Artillery Ground, Finsbury Square 14
Ashley-Cooper, Frederick Samuel 77, 86
Ashton, C.T. 78
Atkins, R.C. 63
Australian tourists 92
Aymes, Adie 148

B

Bacon, F.H. 60
Baigley 20
Bailey, J.A. 133
Bailey, Jim 115
Bailey, W. 18
Baker, H. 69
Baker, Tony 137
Baker, V. 69
Banting, C. 40
Banting, F.
 93, 94, 97, 98, 100, 103, 105, 106, 110

Banting, J. 125, 131
Banting Snr., H.
 40, 44, 45
Barkworth, W.H. 30
Barn Green 52
Barrett, B. 110, 112
Barrett, Colin
 125, 127, 128, 131, 133, 134, 135, 136, 138, 144
Barrett, Ian 135
Barrett, J. 141
Barrett, Maureen 136
Barrett, R.
 105, 111, 112, 115
Barttelo, Sub-Lieut N.J.W. 85
Bass Alton 135
Bastow, Col. 33
Batts, G. 46, 47
Batts, James 29
Bazalgette, Christopher 132, 133, 136
BBC 101, 120
BBC military band 81
BBC South 132
BBC TV 132
Beagley 20
Beagley, E. 40
Beagley, F. 94
Beagley, G. 38
Beagley, George 29
Beagley, Ian 135
Beagley, Marion 29, 147
Beagley, Robert
 30, 103, 108, 112, 115, 125, 129, 135, 136, 143
Beldham, William 13, 28
Bendall 69
Bendall, A. 44, 46
Bendall, C. 100
Best, J.A.
 38, 40, 47, 55, 60
Bishops Waltham 51
Blackman, R. 103
Bligh 27

Bligh, Capt. 22
Blundell, Cecil 102, 104
Blunt, Bruce 82
Boardman, E. 29
Bonham Carter, A.D. 77
Bonham Carter, Major A. 77, 84, 85
Bonham, Henry 16
Bonham, W. 18
Bourne, J. 89
bowling styles 31
Boyce 27
Boyle 22
Bradman, Don 92
Brigands 136
Briggs 69
Brindley, John 140, 141
Broadhalfpenny Cricket Club 75
Broadhalfpenny Down 10
Brockbridge 9
Brook Lane 10, 27
Brown 69
Brown, Bernard
 112, 114, 115, 120, 128
Brown, H.C. 70
Browning, S. 94
Bucksey, Brian
 85, 94, 111
Bucksey, F.H.
 66, 69, 87
Bucksey, Harry 66
Bucksey, J.W. 68
Bucksey, Richard
 66, 69, 81, 85, 97, 103
Budd, H. 46
Budd, W. 44
Bulbeck, John 29
Bulbeck, T. 20, 27, 28
Burdekin, John 148
Bury Lodge 27
Butler, C. 23
Butler Cup
 74, 80, 88, 89, 90, 103
Butler, G.H. 35

– 154 –

Butler, Hew 95, 97
Butler, Major General
   Stephen 98
Butler, S. 23
Butler, T. 29
Butler, T.D. (later Sir
   Thomas)
   22, 23, 33, 36, 38,
   39, 40, 44, 55, 58,
   66, 69, 79, 92
Butler, Thomas 17
Butler, W. 18

C
Caley, M.L. 29, 30
Campbell, Phil 138, 148
Cancellor, Bertram 55
Cannings, Vic 115
Captain Coleridge's XI
   71
Captain Douglas 18
Captain E.J. Ridge 18
Captain Halcott 18
Carson, D. 146, 147
Carson, David 147
Carson, Greg 138
Carter, C. 44
Carter, J. 43
Case 34
Caterham 115, 126
Caterham Spartans
   Cricket Club 106
Cecil Blundell Bat 103
Chakrabati, Indy 148
Chambers, A. 97
Champion, Revd. A.C.
   93, 94, 97, 103
Champness, Sir Thomas
   18
Chaplin, E. 125, 131
Chapman, R. 146
Chase, H. 51
Chase, W. 44
Chester, Rex 115
Chesterfield, C. 91, 94
Chesterfield fielding
   prize 94
Chesterfield, N.A. 91
Chestnut Meadow 27
Clanfield 65

Clanfield parish 10
Clark, Horace 79, 82
Clark, Ted 133
Clay, Major 35
Clay, T. 30
Cobbett, William 22, 24
Col Butler's XI 34
Col C. King 18
Col C. Todd 18
Cole, F. 40
Cole, W. 40
Colles 23
Collis, F. 46, 48, 66
Collis, T. 64, 69
Conan Doyle, A. 42
Cooper, 65
Cooper, Burton F.J.
   64, 65, 69, 70, 74,
   78, 79
Cooper, M.A.L. 85
Coryton, Captain A.F.
   78
Cotman 23
Court, Dr. 51, 52
Courtney, Mr. 39
Cowdrey, Colin 133
Cowie, Commander J.S.
   85
Cricketer Village
   Knock-Out 144
Cricketers Down 23
Crook, C. 40
Crook, F 40
Crook, J. 40
Croydon Cable Works
   87, 89, 90
Cuppage, Lt. Col. 18

D
Dancaster, F. 69
Dancaster, S. 43
Dancaster, W.G. 69
Dartford 13, 115
de Mellow, C.J.
   135, 136, 141, 143
de Mellow, M.G.
   135, 138, 141, 146
Deacon 69
Denmead 9
Denmead Cricket Club 45

Dickenson 22
Dilloway 30
Donaldson, M.J.
   135, 138, 140, 141, 148
Dorset, Duke of 14
Doughty, E.W. 69, 85
Downing College,
   Cambridge 78, 100
Downman, Capt. 27, 33
Doyle, Dr. (A. Conan
   Doyle) 42
Droxford 48
Droxford Parish 34
Droxford station 9
Dunham, Dave
   125, 128, 131
Dunkirk 97
Dunne, A.V. (later Sir
   Vivian) 95
Durrant, E.P. 44
Durrant, W. 49
Dutton, H.S. 35

E
Eagar, E.D.R.
   115, 119, 120, 122, 126,
   127, 134
East Meon 45
Edney 20, 64, 65
Edney, A. 111
Edney, F.O. 64
Engineers Sports 92
Etherington 27
Eton College Servants
   89
Eton Ramblers 79
Extras, Mr. 63

F
Faden, W. 23
Faithful, G.
   97, 98, 103, 110, 135
Faithful, Steve 137, 141
Fareham 2nd XI 44
Farquhar, Lieutenant-
   Commander J.W. 85
Fastrudge 40
Fearon, Venerable W.A.
   58
Fenton, Roger 37

Fiennes, N. 90
First World War 79
Floud, The Rev. H.C.
  46, 52, 55, 63, 65
Foster 23, 27, 28
Foster, J. 36
Foster, John 17, 28, 29
Foster, John Snr 30
Friend 27
Friend, Wm 29
Frogs 89
Fry, C.B.
  56, 58, 64, 133

G

Gage 22
Gale, Fred 27, 28
Gaman 27, 34
Gaman, J. 29, 35, 40
Gaman, Robert 35
Gamman 27
Gannaway, Norman
  17, 27
Gardner, J. 103
Garnier, Rev W. 18
Garrett 27
Gauntlet 23
George Inn 19
Georges, Capt. 23
Gibson, A. 86
Gilliat, Richard 133
Godrich, F. 34
Golding, A. 103
Golding, F. 48
Goldsmith 33
Goldsmith, Commander
  E.P. 79, 85, 86, 89
Goldsmith, E. 42
Goldsmith, J.
  34, 35, 42, 97
Goldsmith, John 29, 30
Goldsmith, Mr. 25
Goodlad, W. 18
Goodwood 23
Goruchi 22
Gosport 34
Grace, W.G. 31, 58
Greatrex 34
Green Lane 9
Green, T. 97

Greentree
  27, 28, 33, 36
Greentree, George
  29, 30
Greyshott 128
Griffinhoofe, R. 18
Griffith, M.G. 133
Gunn, Mr. 40

H

Haig competition 130
Hale, E. 29
Hale, Edward 23
Hale, Major 42
Hale, W. 18
Hall, A. 98, 107
Hall, Albert
  66, 100, 105, 114
Hall, Fred
  78, 86, 89, 90, 91,
  93, 97, 111, 112, 115,
  118
Hall, G.
  63, 66, 69, 87, 98
Hall, Jack 111, 115
Hall, P.M. 78
Hall, R. 135
Hall, W. 36
Hambledon Football
  Club 27
Hambledon Hunt 80
Hambledon Parish 34
Hamilton, Admiral 17
Hamilton, Sir Charles
  19
Hamilton, Sir Edward
  19
Hamilton, W.A. 18
Hammond 27
Hampshire County
  Cricket Club 99
Hampshire Cricket
  Association League
  129
Hampshire Directory 22
Hampshire Eskimos
  80, 82
Hants County Asylum
  64. *See also* Knowle
  Hospital

Harding, S. 103
Harris 28
Harrison, Leo 115
Harrison, R. 90
Harting 35
Hartridge 43
Hartridge, E. 46, 52, 69
Hartridge, F. 42
Hartridge, Geoffrey
  90, 93, 94, 110, 112,
  115, 136
Hartridge, W. 48, 49
Hatfield, W.H. 39
Havant Juniors 43
Haygarth, Arthur 7, 13
Henstridge, W 44
Hesketh Park, Dartford
  115
Higgens 27, 34
Higgens, C 33
Higgens, J.F. 39
Higgens, J.J. 30
Higgens, W. 33, 36
Hill, A.J.L. 78
Hill. Rev. 18
Hinde, Captain 80
Hinton House 34
HMS Mercury 132
HMS Nelson 84
Hobbs, Jack 57
Hodges, Admiral Sir
  H.M. 86
Hodgson, N. 36
Holmes, F. 43
Hooker 46, 68, 85
Hooker, H.
  40, 46, 87, 90, 94,
  104, 107, 111
Hooker, J. 66
Hopkins, Jesse 56, 60
Horn, Dr. 87
Horn, S. 133
Horndean 44
Horndean Cricket Club
  40
HRH Prince Edward of
  Wales 58
Hughes, A. 49
Humphrey 33
Humphrey, E. 35

– 156 –

Humphrey, W. 36, 38
Hunsdonbury 37
Hunt, I. 38
Hurst, F. 46
Hyde Abbey House 19
Hyde, Edward 45
Hyde Ramblers CC 128
Hyde, Sir Nicholas 45

I

Idsworth 47
Ingleby-Mackenzie,
  Colin 115, 120, 121

J

Jackman, F. 33, 35
James, J. 125, 128, 131
James, S. 141
James, Simon 148
Jarman 23
Jarman, H. 29
Jephson, Rev. W.V. 59
Jeram, Dr. 44
Jerram 20
Jessop, Captain 29
Jessop, Gilbert 58, 59
Johnston, Brian 138
Jones, G.H. 30
Jones, Matt 148
Jones, Richard 135
Joyce, J. 46

K

Kelsall 22
Kelsey 23
Kenway, Derek 148
Kenway, R. 146
Khurana, Mannish 149
King Edward VIII 58
Kingsley, Sir Patrick 77
Knight 23
Knight, A.E. 77
Knight, C.W. 65
Knight, G.M. 38
Knight, J.
  44, 47, 49, 66, 72
Knight, Major 111
Knight, Ronald 22
Knowle Hospital 87, 90
Kumar Shri Ranjitsinjhi 56

L

ladies team 145
Lady Butler Cup
  94, 105, 107, 116, 118
Lake Barton, Revd John 34
Lang, W. 38
Langridge junior, W. 66
Langridge, W.
  43, 46, 48, 49, 52,
  56, 64, 74, 79, 85
Langrish, W. 30
Langtree 23
Laurence, A. 18
Lawrence, E. 106
Lay 40
le Clercq, A. 141
le Clercq, Mark
  135, 137, 138, 140, 149
Lee, E.C. 79
Lee, T. 44
Leigh Park 51
Lewis, Colonel 87
Lewis, Dr. 102, 103
Lilley, Len 120
Littlefield 23
Loraine 33
Lord Saye and Seale 90
Lord, Thomas 14
Lords 140
Lowndes, W.G.
  78, 87, 119
Lucas, E.V. 28, 35, 77
Lunn 33
Lunn, D. 29
Lunn, E. 43, 44
Lunn, E.F.W. 44
Lunn, S. 33, 36
Lunn, Sidney 29, 31
Lutyens, Charles
  132, 135, 136

M

Macdonell, A.G. 81
Macey 81, 85
Macey, F.
  74, 79, 80, 82, 85
Magrath, Adrian
  133, 135, 136, 141, 149
Mann, Sir Horatio 14

March, E. 43
Marchant, L. 128
Marchant, Len
  125, 127, 128, 131
Married v. Single 34
Marshall, Roy 115
Martin, Capt. 33
Marylebone 11
Marylebone Cricket
  Club 14
Mason, Alan 131, 133
May, A.J.
  43, 46, 98, 102, 103
May, C. 72
May, E.A. 85
May, H. 40, 125
May, Mavis 111
May, Philip
  105, 107, 110, 111, 112
May, Rudevic 84
May, W. 40
Maynard, Rev W. 40
McDonell, H.C. 78
memorial 55
Meon Valley 9, 52
Meredith 20, 27
Meredith, F. 34, 36
Meredith, H. 38
Merrington, K. 103
Milburne, Colin 133
Miller, D. 90
Miller, J. 133
Monckton, Walter 82
Money Values 5
monument 10
Moon, A. 72
Moon, G. 66
Moon, K.
  105, 107, 110, 111, 112,
  120, 131
Mote, Ashley 14, 55, 77
Munro Hall, Rolf 136
Munton, G. 133
Munton, R.
  125, 128, 131
Murphy, A. 135

N

Newland, A. 80, 85, 87
Newland, L. 69

Newland, R. 66, 69
Newland, W.A. 85
Newman, Jack 59, 63
Newman, R. 133
Nichol, Mr. 104
Noel Fisher Knock-out 137, 144
Nondescripts 89, 95
Norris, R. 147
North End Business Men 87
North Stoneham 86
Nyren, John 32, 120
Nyren, R.P. 112
Nyren, Richard 10, 15, 38

O

O'Donnell, B.W. 81
Officers of the Club 150
Orange, Lieut. 33
Oxford Gazette and Reading Mercury 13

P

Pain, Thomas 16
Palmer, Ed 44
Paris, Cecil 134, 137
Park House 17
Parr, George 31
Parvin 43
Parvin, Arthur Edward 68
Parvin, F. 46
Parvin, Godfrey 66, 69, 71, 72, 74, 78, 79, 80, 81
Parvin, P. 103, 107, 111, 112
Parvin, R. 103
Parvin, S. 103
Pask, G. 135
Patteson, Revd T. 29
pavilion, new 123
Pay 27
Pay, Colin 140, 141
Pease family 55
Peggott, C. 66
Penny, Mr. 46
Peters, A.B. 81

Petersfield District Association of Umpires 128
Pink 27, 28
Pink, G. 29
Pink, George 29
Pink, H. 66
Pink, R. 29
Pipon, Lieut. 33
Poole 20
Poole, F. 33, 36
Poole, Mr. 98
Portchester 90
Portsmouth Amateurs 89
Portsmouth Electricity 103
Portsmouth Grammar School 90
Portsmouth Rugby Club 51
Portsmouth Transport 103
Poulter 22
Powlett, Mr. 13
Poynings 139
Purbrook 43
Purdey, W.M. 18
Pycroft, James 13

R

Ranjitsinjhi, Kumar Shri 56, 57
Rapsom, W.G. 43
Rashleigh, Mr. 21
Reading Mercury 13
Regency Cricket Club of Brighton 100
Repton School 77
Richards 22
Richards, Rev. G. 18, 21
Richardson, A.W. 77
Ridge Meadow 10, 27, 87, 108, 122, 129, 140, 146, 147, 148
Ridge, T. 29
Ridge. T. J. 19
Ridgewell, G. 115
Robertson-Glasgow, R.C. 78, 87

Robson, Lieut. 33
Roe, Dr. 69
Rosier, Henry 30
Rowe, Becky 145
Royal Artillery 34, 37, 48
Royal Marines 34
Royal Naval School of Music 71
Royle, G. 38
Rutledge, F. 69, 79

S

Sabin, P. 51, 52
Salters of Winchester 58
Sandover 33
Satterthwaite, Lieutenant-Commander E.S. 85
Sayner, W. 95, 97, 118
Sealey, F. 52
Shawyer, A. 103
Sherreff, S. 147
Shotton, Gary 149
Simpson, Lieutenant-Commander G.W.G. 85
Sims, Steve 135
Singleton, F. 51
Slowe, W 40
Small, Greg 138, 145
Smith 22
Smith, Allan 149
Smith, C. 40
Smith, J. 90, 91, 93, 95, 103
Smith, Thomas Assheton 19
Smith, Tom 13, 19, 25
Snow, E.E. 17
Soberton 51
Solomon, Harry 145
South Hants Cricket Club 27
Southern League 144
Southern Television 120
Southsea Rovers 42
Southsea Wanderers 86, 90, 95
Southwick 103, 104

Sparshot 69
Speltham Hill 9
Spinks, Sergt. 33
Sprot, E.M. 58, 60
Squire, J.C (Sir John) 80
Steel, Marina 145, 149
Stent, L. 103
Stephenson, D. 133
Stevens. J.E. 85
Stevenson, J.B. 42
Stewart 23
Straus, R. 81
Strong Cup 130

T
Tandy 33
Tanner, T.
　107, 110, 111
Tanner, W.
　40, 97, 103, 105, 112
Tanner, W.G. 110, 111
Taylor, D. 125
Taylor, M. 103
Taylor, W. 40
Tew, A.M. 77
The Bat and Ball
　10, 80, 126
The George Inn 10, 38
The Green Man 9
The New Inn
　10, 51, 79
The Vine Inn 10
Thompson, J. 131
Thornycroft, Hamo 55
Thresher 34
Tolchard, Roger 147
Tomkins, Peter
　125, 133, 135, 136, 138
Toogood, Lieut. 33
Training Ship Mercury
　58
Trasenster, Major W.A.
　78
Triangular Tournament
　57
Trojans 143
Tuke, Major J.M. 85

Tupper, Lieut. 33
Turner, Alf 69
Turner, Chris
　72, 80, 87, 89, 90,
　91, 93, 94, 97, 98,
　103, 105, 107, 111
Turner, H. (Stumps)
　44, 46, 66, 84, 88
Turner, Ian
　135, 138, 142, 149
Turner, J.E.
　66, 79, 82, 98, 99,
　102, 104, 106, 107, 114
Turner, Jacqueline 145
Turner, Jim 69
Turner, Robert (Topsy)
　44, 114, 117, 125, 127,
　128, 130, 131, 133, 135,
　137, 140, 149
Turner, Ron
　100, 103, 107, 110, 111,
　112, 114, 115, 120, 125,
　127, 128, 129, 130, 134,
　136, 141, 143
Tusler, Phil 147, 149
Twynam, J. 43
Twynam, W. 48

U
Underwood, Derek 147

V
van Deinsen, Bret 145

W
Wadhams 94
Wallace, George
　93, 94, 95, 98
Walter, W. 38
War Memorial 68
Ware, R.
　107, 108, 110, 115
Ware, W. 125
Waterloo 47
Waterloo Park 33
Waterlooville 9
Watson, Admiral
　111, 112, 115

Watson, Captain F.B. 85
Watson, J.
　89, 94, 97, 98, 103,
　104
Weekes, D.V. 115
West Indians 94
Whalley-Tooker,
　Dorothy 119
Whalley-Tooker, Edward
　45, 46, 49, 55, 56,
　60, 64, 65, 66, 67,
　69, 72, 78, 79, 81,
　83, 85, 87, 89, 90,
　91, 92, 94, 97, 138
Whalley-Tooker, Hyde
　45, 71, 78
Whalley-Tooker, Hyde
　Charnock 66, 69
White, Bob 136
White Conduit Club 14
White, Lieutenant R.T.
　(Dick) 84, 85
White, Sir Archibald 84
Whittenham, A. 38
Wiggington 48
Williams, W. 69
Willoughby, F.G. 40
Willsher, Edgar 32
Wilson, J.A. 69
Wilson, Rockley 77
Wilson, T.H. 35
Winchester 9
Winchester College
　14, 75, 77
Winchilsea 14
Winchilsea, Earl of
　14, 17
Windmill Down
　7, 8, 10, 14, 17
Wingham, Mark
　133, 135, 137, 146, 149
Wisden, John 31
Woodger 43
Worsley 22
Wren, E.F. 69, 79
Wright, W.K. 40
Wyatt, R.E.S. 120
Wyndham 34

Other books by Neil Jenkinson

C.P. Mead - Hampshire's Greatest Run-maker. Paul Cave, Southampton, 1992

A History of Peter Symonds', 1993

Cricket's Greatest Comeback Hampshire v. Warwickshire 1922. John Mckenzie, Ewell, 1998

Images of Sport, Hampshire County Cricket Club (With Dave Allen and Andrew Renshaw), Tempus Publications Limited, Stroud, 2000

END